Past-into-Present Series

SHIPS AND SHIPPING

Michael Palmer

Senior History Master
Rickmansworth Grammar School

B. T. BATSFORD LTD London

First published 1971
© M. D. Palmer, 1971

Filmset by Keyspools Ltd, Golborne, Lancs.

Printed in Great Britain by Billing & Sons Ltd, Guildford, Surrey
for the Publishers
B. T. Batsford Ltd, 4 Fitzhardinge Street, London W1

7134 1767 6

Acknowledgment

The illustration on page 20 is reproduced by gracious permission of Her Majesty the Queen.

The author and publishers would also like to thank the following for permission to reproduce other illustrations which appear in this book:

Messrs. Allen and Unwin Ltd. and Bokforlaget Forum, Stockholm for fig. 21; Britannia Royal Naval College, Dartmouth, for fig. 5; British Petroleum Co. Ltd. for figs. 50, 62; Cunard Steam-Ship Co. Ltd. for fig. 30; W. Cuthbertson Esq. for fig. 14; Esso Petroleum Co. Ltd. for fig. 61; Hythe Public Library for fig. 6; Imperial War Museum for figs. 42, 43, 45, 47; Keystone Press Agency for fig. 39; Lloyds of London for fig. 34; Manchester Ship Canal Co. for fig. 59; Mansell Collection for fig. 16; Museum of History of Science, Oxford, for fig. 8; National Maritime Museum for figs. 7a, 7b, 9, 11, 12, 13, 15, 18, 19, 20, 27, 28, 29, 31, 37; Popperfoto for figs. 32, 46, 48, 49, 51, 53, 60; Port of London Authority for figs. 54, 56, 57, 63, 64; Radio Times Hulton Picture Library for figs. 2, 33, 35, 36, 38, 41, 55, 58; Science Museum for figs. 23, 24, 25; Skyfotos for fig. 40; South East Press Agency for fig. 52; John Stobart for fig. 26; Thornton and Butterworth Ltd. for fig. 44, from *The World Crisis 1916–18*, by W. S. Churchill.

Contents

List of Illustrations

1 Early Trade

The earliest method of water carriage was by rafts or floating logs, but these cannot be classed as ships, as they support weight merely through the buoyancy of the materials. A form of water transport becomes a ship when it supports weight through its displacement of water. Ships emerged, therefore, when early man began to hollow out logs with a flint, and to cover a framework of wood with skins to form a canoe. In some areas, particularly in Ecuador, rafts made of balsa wood and fitted with sails were used until quite recent times. That they were capable of ocean voyages was proved by some Norwegian scientists who sailed such a raft, called the Kon-Tiki, from South America to the islands east of Tahiti. In Europe, however, the ship developed very early. It was before 3000 B.C. that the Egyptians first harnessed the wind to provide the motive power for water transport through the use of a mast and sails. They did not travel very far for general trade; perhaps they went as far as Tyre and Sidon for the tight-grained cedar wood, but more usually they went to the Sinai desert across the Red Sea for copper. The expedition which Queen Hatshepsut of Egypt sent to the land of Punt, which is thought to be in the vicinity of modern Mozambique, was probably very unusual.

Apart from Egypt, the most advanced centres of civilisation were on the Fertile Crescent between the Persian Gulf and Palestine, and therefore the most advanced shipping was to be found in the Mediterranean. Little is known of the Cretans, who were the dominant sea power around 1500 B.C., but it seems that already they were differentiating between rowing galleys, which were favoured for war purposes, and sailing ships which were more suitable for trade. They were superseded by the Phoenicians, who based their small mercantile Empire on the city ports of Acre, Tyre and Sidon. The Phoenicians had few interests outside trade and were intrepid travellers. They traded their glassware and purple garments with Spain in exchange for silver, and with the Britons in exchange for tin. In 822 B.C. they settled at Carthage and thereafter became known as Carthaginians. They dominated the trade of the Mediterranean world and also began to explore the coast of Africa.

Their contribution to the development of shipping was the bireme, which was a vessel with two banks of oars on each side. The reason for this arrangement was the difficulty of extending the length of a galley, which was a narrow, shallow craft with a tendency to sag and break in the middle if it was too long. This oar formation was first introduced in 700 B.C., and during the next 500 years successful boats were developed with three banks of oars called triremes, and even with five banks called quinquiremes. It was the Greeks who were responsible for the latter

5

ship. They were a great seafaring people who also developed the standard hull of a sailing ship which is carvel built. Carvel means that the planks are flush with each other on the framework of the hull so that it has a smooth finish, as opposed to clinker-built where the planking overlaps to give the hull a stepped finish.

The Carthaginians also introduced the ram on the front of their galleys for use in war, but this weapon was turned on them by the Romans who built a fleet of 120 warships in 60 days, using a captured Carthaginian war galley as a model. Not only did the Romans provide their ships with rams, but they also added drawbridges that were held to the mast by pulleys. These were allowed to fall onto the Carthaginian ships, and a heavy spike at the end pierced the enemy's deck, holding the ships together. In this way the naval battle off the coast of Sicily became more like a land battle, with the Roman soldiers, led by their consul, Dullius, swarming over the ladders into the Carthaginian ships. This battle took place in 242 B.C.

The Romans carried on the African trade after their defeat of the Carthaginians. Nowhere was the diversity of Roman trade more obvious than at Alexandria, a great city in Egypt founded by Alexander the Great in 332 B.C. but later captured by Rome. The basic trade was in the export of heavy commodities such as wine and olive oil in exchange for corn, but all the luxury products of the East such as silk and spices were on sale there. The canal link between the Mediterranean Sea

1 A Roman merchant ship of the second century A.D. Notice the second sail on the bow mast and the paddle-shaped rudders on each side of the ship.

and the Indian Ocean was of great antiquity. Herodotus the historian, writing in about 440 B.C. said, 'It was Necos who began the construction of the canal to the Arabian Gulf, a work afterwards completed by Darius the Persian. The length of the canal is four days' journey by boat and its breadth sufficient to allow two triremes to be rowed abreast.' Alexandria also possessed one of the wonders of the world in the form of the Pharos, a great lighthouse, 480 feet high with a fire of resinous wood giving warning to shipping.

The Romans were great engineers themselves and they built docks as well as the more publicised roads. Ptolemy, who was a Greek living in Alexandria, claimed that the roads radiating from Rome were so well graded that 'a wagon could take the weight of a barge'. He was not, however, seeking to prove that road transport was superior to shipping. The Roman roads were good, but the great advantage of sea carriage still remained that far less power is needed to move a load suspended in water than is needed to move it over land.

There were some important refinements to ship design during Roman times. Roman ships had far deeper hulls, to cope with their heavy loads, compared with the shallow-draught Phoenician ships. They also added a second sail on a short mast jutting out at an angle over the bow, and two large paddle-shaped rudders on each side of the ship.

Arab shipping in the Indian Ocean was well advanced. After 50 A.D. the Arabs began to exploit the discovery by the Greek sea captain Hippalos, that the monsoon winds provided a rapid and reliable means of power direct across the ocean to peninsular India, which made the old coastal route obsolete. The Arabs employed a triangular sail on their boats, as they still do; this sail is far more versatile than the square sail as it can be trimmed to receive wind on either side, and enables the boat to be sailed much closer to the wind. It was once presumed that the Arabs, and the Muslim conquest of North Africa and of the Middle East between 600 and 700 A.D., were mainly responsible for the adoption of the triangular sail in the Mediterranean, but it now seems that it began to be introduced during the Roman period in the second century A.D. It gradually replaced the square sail completely in the Mediterranean and was named the lateen sail in reference to the Latin people who used it. Many ships of this kind must have visited England towards the end of the Roman occupation, which lasted from 43 A.D. to 410 A.D.

The Vikings
After the collapse of the Roman Empire in the West in the fifth century A.D., and the conquest of North Africa and Spain by the Muslim Arabs in the seventh century, the main routes of European trade were disrupted and the towns, which had developed for the exchange of goods, began to decline. It was the Vikings who started trade again. They lived in Norway, Sweden and Denmark and began as marauding pirates, but later settled in places as far apart as England, Normandy,

7

2 This Viking ship was discovered at Gokstad, Norway, in an almost perfect state of preservation. It dates from the ninth century.

Russia and Sicily. In England, they settled in the Danelaw after Guthrum's treaty with Alfred in 879 A.D., and a little before they had been invited to rule over the Slav tribes in Russia. They were variously known as Danes, Northmen or Norsemen and their enterprise enabled them to trade with Byzantium (now called Istanbul), the great capital of the Eastern Roman Empire, by way of the Baltic Sea and the Russian Rivers flowing into the Black Sea. They exchanged furs, honey and slaves for the luxury silks, brocades and gold lamés which had come from Byzantium trade with the East. The Viking long ships were rudimentary boats in comparison with the elaborate rowing craft of the Ancient World in the Mediterranean, but they did contribute to the development of the typical European sailing ship. They were shallow draught galleys that could penetrate up the river estuaries with ease. Examples dating from the ninth century have been unearthed from the peat of Norway in a good state of preservation, and it is clear that they had both sails and a single bank of oars. They had various points of difference from Mediterranean craft. Their steering board was on one side of the boat only and this side was called the steerboard or starboard. Their main characteristic, however, was that they were clinker-built and were double-ended in the sense that the stern was almost exactly similar to the bow. The bow and stern rose high in the air and were elaborately carved, often to represent a snake's or dragon's head.

The Normans who conquered England in 1066 were descended from the Norsemen, and therefore the ships in which William the Conqueror's army came were very similar to Viking longships. The only improvement was in the framework which was now built round a true keel. In the 12th century, the northern ship was brought closer to its southern counterpart by the introduction of stern rudder, which not only gave much more efficient steering, but also made it necessary to differentiate the bow from the stern. Another development at this time was the supporting of the mast by stays, which strengthened it and made possible the inclusion of a fighting top or crow's nest above the sail. Temporary structures, called forecastles and sterncastles, were also built at bow and stern to give the bowmen a fighting platform in battle.

Medieval Trade

The revival of Mediterranean trade was associated with the fortunes of Venice, which had started as a village of fishermen living on the lagoons off the coast of North Italy and had gradually established a coastal trade with Byzantium. Byzantium had never developed a fleet of its own and it was to depend on Norsemen or Venetians for its trade. Venice's emergence as the greatest city of the

3 This sketch of the portion of the Bayeux tapestry showing William the Conqueror's crossing from Normandy to Pevensey in Sussex in 1066, shows that his ships were almost identical to Viking longboats. Shields were arranged along the gunwale to give added protection.

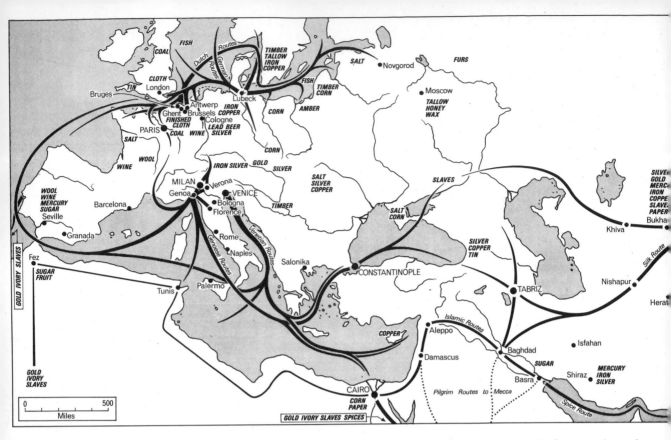

4 Medieval trade routes. This map illustrates the importance of the North Sea as a place where trade routes met. The most important centre was still North Italy, where the cities of Venice and Genoa dominated the trade in luxury goods with Asia.

Mediterranean occurred when the Crusaders established feudal kingdoms in Palestine and Syria (1099), and Christians were able to trade direct with the ports of the Eastern Mediterranean which had links with the Indian and Chinese trade. Venice, together with Genoa and Pisa to a lesser extent, also benefited from the decline of Byzantine trade with Russia due to the settlement of the Kipchak Turks in southern Russia. From the 12th century onwards, these Italian ports were able to monopolize Mediterranean trade, especially after Venice sacked the city of Byzantium during the so-called 4th Crusade in 1204. Venice had double access to the products of the East either by way of the overland route to China, the 'Silk Road', which Marco Polo followed during his travels (1271–1291), or by way of the sea route, the 'Pepper road', by way of the Red Sea and the Indian Ocean (although there was now no canal link between the Mediterranean and the Red Sea). By 1381, Venice had destroyed the fleet of her main rival, Genoa, and really ruled the Sea.

The new route to Northern Europe was from the North Italian ports over the Alps to the Rhine valley and thence to Flanders. Flanders was also the natural meeting point for the trade of the Baltic ports and the Mediterranean by sea, and it was here that the great medieval port of Bruges developed. This new link with the south also benefited London, which, though it was never the equal of Bruges or Venice, still had great commercial importance and was, in time, to become the greatest port in the world.

London was by far the most important port in England, but the merchants of London did not have much control over the trade of Northern Europe. The principal routes were dominated by the Hanseatic League, which was a trading association of the North German towns. It was formed in 1241 by the cities of Lubeck, Cologne and Hamburg and grew to include as many as 80 towns in the vicinity of North Germany, many of them well inland. The English economy depended on one product, wool, and it was therefore important to find as many markets as possible. Medieval kings were therefore, on the whole, pleased to welcome the Hanse and to allow them to establish a warehouse in London called the Steelyard. The Hanse brought furs, corn, pitch, wax and timber which they exchanged for wool. English wool found a ready market in Flanders and it soon became clear that it could be easily managed by English merchants and become a valuable source of customs income. The Company of the Staple was given the monopoly of wool exports by Edward I and eventually established itself at Calais. There was one exception to their monopoly and this was the right of Venetians and Florentines to export wool to Italy. A monopoly is the exclusive right to market a certain article or to trade with a certain area, and most medieval companies were given such rights when they were given the royal charter.

The development of the native cloth industry in the late Middle Ages led to the decline in the exports of raw wool. All England needed was to learn the weaving

5 Bruges. This painting by Hendrick van Minderhout shows the port of Bruges with the city in the background. It was the busiest commercial centre in Northern Europe during the Middle Ages. Minderhout began living at Bruges in 1652, so this painting represents Bruges after its golden age had passed.

6 The seal of the port of Hythe, which shows a medieval ship that is as simple as a Viking longboat, but with fore and stern castles and a deeper draught. Hythe was one of the five original Cinque ports (the others were Hastings, Romsey, Dover and Sandwich). The Cinque ports were a confederacy of towns for mutual defence and for co-operation in the North Sea fishery. The confederacy was recognized by the Crown in the thirteenth century and often supplied ships for the King's use.

skill from the Flemish tradesman, as there were plenty of fast streams where fulling mills could be built to provide the machinery for the cleansing and the thickening of the cloth. The one skill they did not readily develop was that of dyeing and finishing, which was still mainly left to the Flemish weavers. In the cloth trade with the Netherlands there emerged a group of English merchants who became known as the Merchant Adventurers. By 1450, the whole trade in cloth was monopolized by them and they were granted privileges by the Duke of Burgundy in the port of Antwerp. Antwerp became the great market place for English cloth and English trade was more or less concentrated on the London-Antwerp route.

There was not much English enterprise outside these short routes. Geoffrey Chaucer describes in his Prologue to the *Canterbury Tales*, a Dartmouth skipper, who was part privateer and part trader. He stole wine from the vintners at Bordeaux and allowed a dagger to hang freely on a lanyard from his neck, yet he was a very skilled navigator:

> *As for his skill in reckoning his tides,*
> *Currents and many another risk besides,*
> *Moons, harbours, pilots, he had such dispatch*
> *That none from Hull to Carthage was his match.*
> *Hardy he was, prudent in undertaking;*
> *His beard in many a tempest had its shaking,*
> *And he knew all the havens as they were*
> *From Gottland to the Cape of Finisterre,*
> *And every creek in Brittany and Spain.*

Despite this enterprise in the outports, English trade was dominated by London and partly operated by foreigners. In 1485, almost a half of English trade was carried by foreign ships, many belonging to the Hanse. The Italian fleets, now composed of large carracks, still arrived at Southampton each year to fetch a supply of English wool. English shipping had not yet emerged.

7 Two pictures showing caravels. The unique contemporary drawing (above) shows Dover harbour at the time of Henry VIII. The caravels were the typical merchant ship of the time. The line engraving (below) of 1566 shows the positions of the sails when a caravel sailed close to the wind.

The Caravel

By 1300, the appearance of the English ship was changing, as oars were dispensed with and the castles at bow and stern were incorporated into the design of the ship. A small bowsprit was also brought into use, not apparently to support a sprit sail, but to help to raise the anchor. Ships were still quite small until 1400; the largest were probably no more than 300 tons. In the following hundred years ship design developed apace and by 1500, ships of 1,000 tons were common.

The evidence suggests that in 1400 the northern ship was still one-masted with a square sail and was entirely incapable of making headway against an adverse wind. It would therefore have to remain in port awaiting favourable weather. Meanwhile the Mediterranean ship had made very little progress since Roman times, except for the use of lateen sails and more than one mast. The caravel was developed by the Portuguese, who were ideally situated to incorporate the best in ship design from both south and north. The caravel had three masts, two rigged for square sails and the rear or mizzen mast for a lateen sail. The square sails gave great driving power, while the lateen gave the ability to make headway against an adverse wind. This was the ship that enabled Portugal to explore the coast of Africa; it was also the ship in which Columbus sailed to America. The *Santa Maria*, in fact, had three masts and five sails; the two additional ones were the spritsail, set forward beneath the bowsprit, a spar on which no sail had been set since Roman times, and the small topsail, which was set above the mainsail.

The caravel, which as its name suggests has a carvel hull, was known in England by 1450, and thereafter English navigators had a ship which was capable of sailing the oceans. The opening up of the world, in the main, was left to Portugal and Spain, but a Genoese called John Cabot did sail from Bristol in 1497 under the patronage of Henry VII to discover lands to the West. It is also alleged that Henry VII might have had the chance of employing Columbus, who spent a long time looking for a government to finance him. England, therefore, was not completely inactive while the world was discovered.

Navigational Instruments

Until the 16th century, European ships never ventured far from land. They had carried compasses at least since the 13th century, and therefore had some idea of direction, but they had no scientific method of fixing their position out of sight of land until the end of the 15th century. It was a prince of Portugal, called Henry the Navigator, who began to make available the advanced geography of the Greeks, and the exact knowledge of astronomy of the Arabs, to the seamen he was sending out to explore the coast of Africa. They began to plot their position latitude by the Pole Star at night and by the sun by day. Navigation by the sun is particularly complicated, for it is in a different position in the heavens every day and seamen need a special almanac containing tables of the sun's movement. The position longitude was found by assessing the distance travelled in a longitudinal direction. This was done by measuring the speed of the ship by means

8   An astrolabe. This was the instrument used by navigators to plot their position latitude by the stars at night. This particular example was made in England about the year 1370.

of a rope, knotted at regular intervals and attached to a piece of wood, which was allowed to run out over the stern for a certain period of time measured by a sand-glass. The number of knots that passed over the side of the ship were counted and the sea speed was expressed in knots, as it has been ever since.

Another weakness of medieval navigation was the lack of accurate maps. It was not until the 16th century that maps were devised with lines of latitude and longitude shown as straight lines on a regular projection. Earlier sailors had their own free hand maps called portolani, which they drew up from their own sailing experience. They normally showed the coastline with its bays and headlands and included a network of lines to show the direction from place to place. They covered most of the European coastline, but were based on the supposition that the ship would not lose sight of land for long.

There were great improvements in navigational aids in the 16th century. When it was realised that Columbus's discovery was not part of Asia, and the extent of the Pacific Ocean was proved by Magellan, the Greek ideas described in Ptolemy's *Geography*, which had been the most advanced ideas of the world since 130 A.D., were finally set aside. Reasonably accurate maps of the explored regions of the globe were published in the second half of the 16th century by Gerard Mercator, who also introduced a method of map projection. New navigational instruments appeared to replace the astrolobe for taking readings of the sun and stars; the cross-staff, the back-staff and the quadrant were all used. It was these aids which enabled navigators to sail the oceans with increasing confidence.

The Antwerp Trade

From the point of view of English merchants, there was a good reason why they did not venture far, and that was the proximity of the essential outlets for their trade. There was an attempt by Henry VII (1485–1509) to open up trading outlets other than the Netherlands for English trade, to Danzig in the Baltic Sea, to Tuscany in the Mediterranean and to Bergen in Norway. He also emulated Spain and Portugal by encouraging John Cabot to search for a North-West Passage to China. Cabot sailed from Bristol in the *Matthew* in 1497 with 18 persons and if he did not find a route to China, he did discover the fishing banks off Newfoundland teeming with cod. Yet none of these openings was exploited in the next fifty years.

The reason for the lack of enterprise of English traders in exploiting these openings was that there was an almost insatiable demand for English broad cloth at the port of Antwerp, and there was no incentive to look elsewhere. Antwerp became the focus for European trade once the Portuguese had opened up a new route to India round the Cape of Good Hope, which by-passed the Mediterranean. The Portuguese brought their spices to Antwerp where they could be exchanged for the products of the Baltic Sea or for English cloth. It soon also became a magnet for all European goods, such as the silks and satins of Italy and the linen and metal goods of Germany.

By the middle of the 16th century the English economy had become dangerously dependent on one manufactured article, cloth, and one outlet, Antwerp. At Antwerp the cloth was exchanged for a very wide selection of imports from all over Europe. The author of a book called the *Commonweal of this Realm of England*, written about 1550, drew attention to the new consumption of foreign goods: 'I have seen within these 20 years, when there were not a dozen of these haberdashers who sell French or Milan caps, glasses, daggers, swords and such things in all London. And now from the Tower to Westminster along, every street is full of them.'

England's dependence on Antwerp was so great that it was essential that good relations were maintained with the rulers of the Netherlands. From 1516 onwards, the Netherlands and Spain were ruled by the same king, who also was elected Holy Roman Emperor in 1519 as Emperor Charles v. It was therefore of the first importance that Spain, and Charles v, remained friendly, not only for the sake of the Antwerp market but also for the important direct trade that England carried on with Spain. This was particularly difficult for religious reasons, for while Spain was fervently Catholic, England was undergoing a Reformation which began with the nullification of Henry viii's marriage to Catherine of Aragon, Charles v's aunt.

As there was a danger that Spain might ban English traders from Antwerp, as happened in 1545, England was glad to allow the Hanseatic League to carry English cloth from London to Antwerp, so that they would maintain the trade in troubled times. The short route to Antwerp also gave no incentive to shippers to acquire large ships. Smaller craft like the two-masted ketches and the one-masted hoys and doggers were perfectly capable of crossing the Channel or the North Sea. They were always an important, but unspectacular, part of English shipping, carrying coal from Newcastle to London or transporting cloth from London to Flanders. For these reasons, the great period of Antwerp was also the lowest point for English merchant shipping.

The dangers of concentrating on one export commodity like cloth were revealed in 1551, when there was a catastrophic slump in cloth demand after a period of overproduction. Everyone connected with cloth, from the sheep-farmer producing the wool to the cottage spinner and the cottage weaver, suffered. It became clear that English merchants would either have to find new markets for cloth or new commodities which they could sell to make a living. The willingness of English investors to risk their money in adventurous expeditions increased after 1551, and by the end of Elizabeth's reign in 1603 attempts had been made to market a number of new commodities, not always successfully. Many of these articles, such as furs, fish, slaves and timber were to become the basis of many prosperous trades in the next two centuries.

What made these searches all the more urgent was the decline of Antwerp as a great port for religious and political reasons. From 1563 onwards, the Netherlands increasingly resisted attempts by the Spanish authorities to eradicate Protestantism and to increase Spanish control. Antwerp became a focus for violence, first at the hands of Protestant image-breakers who wrecked the city in 1566, and secondly at the hands of unpaid Spanish soldiers who destroyed the city in 1576. In fact, the Merchant Adventurers ceased to use Antwerp as their trading centre as early as 1564, when the Spanish once again forbade English imports. They moved around Northern Europe searching for a base and finally settled in Middleburg, in the North Netherlands, in 1598.

Trade Expansion

The traditional English broadcloth was a warm, practical material, rather coarse in texture and dyed only in plain colours, if at all. It was not a commodity which could easily be sold, especially in warmer countries. It was therefore fortunate that Flemish immigrants from the Netherlands, fleeing from Spanish persecution, brought with them their skills in making the 'new draperies', which were much lighter and more attractive. These lighter cloths, which were called bays and says, were sold in the Mediterranean countries, and by 1600 were beginning to sell well in the traditional broad cloth areas.

Most of the expeditions that set out after 1551 were looking for quick profits rather than a regular trade. This was particularly the case with expeditions to the north, which were lured by the hope of finding a new route to China. China, or Cathay as it was called, was a land of fabulous riches which every trader hoped to reach. The Muscovy Company sent Hugh Willoughby and Richard Chancellor to search for a North-East passage to China in 1553. Willoughby and his crew died from cold off the North Cape, but Chancellor found his way to the White Sea and from there he journeyed to Moscow by sleigh. In this way, the Muscovy Company opened up a trade with Russia in furs, hemp and tallow, which was exclusively English. Equal enterprise was shown by Martin Frobisher (1576–78) and John Davis (1585–87) in searching for a North-West passage, but without the same commercial result. It was Henry Hudson's discovery of Hudson Bay in 1610, even though Hudson himself and his son were tragically left to perish in an open boat by a mutinying crew, that opened up an even more successful fur trade.

Changes in the political situation in the Baltic and Mediterranean Sea led to the expansion of English trade. The Hanseatic League was under increasing pressure from 1552 onwards to extend to English traders in the Baltic the same privileges as they themselves enjoyed in London. These were begrudgingly granted in 1560 and English trade grew when the individual English traders formed themselves into the Eastland Company in 1578. Their trade was in timber, cordage, and pitch, all of which were vital to ship-building and became essential for the growth of the English ship-building industry in the next 250 years.

The Mediterranean Sea was closed to English shipping during the period of Turkish Muslim naval supremacy from 1520–1571. This Turkish domination, which troubled all Christian Europe, was ended by Spain, who defeated the Turks at Lepanto in the Gulf of Corinth in the last major galley battle of history in 1571. By 1578, English traders had permission to trade with the Turkish Empire, and in 1581 formed themselves into the Levant Company to trade in luxuries such as silk and porcelain.

The rest of the world had been divided between Spain and Portugal under the terms of the Treaty of Tordesillas, 1494, with Pope Alexander VI as arbiter. An imaginary line was drawn in the Atlantic to divide the Spanish lands in the West from the Portuguese lands in the East. This left Portugal with the true route to India round the Cape of Good Hope. These arrangements did not deter English enterprise. It was possible for private individuals to be in a state of war with Spain in the colonies without affecting the situation in Europe overmuch. John Hawkins attempted to open up a legitimate trade in slaves with the Spanish Empire between 1562 and 1567. They were in great demand among the Spanish planters, who were prepared to exchange slaves for sugar, but it contravened Spanish colonial policy. Although the trade was ended in 1568 after Hawkins' ships had been savaged by a Spanish fleet at St. Jean de Uloa, the slave trade was to become very important during the next two centuries.

After 1568, English merchants took to privateering against the Spanish treasure fleet, and Francis Drake, at least, had astonishing success first on the Isthmus of Panama in 1572, and then in the Pacific ports of Peru during his

9 Francis Drake (1540–1596). Drake was the leading English privateer in the reign of Elizabeth and was responsible for the most daring exploits against the Spanish silver trade. On the *Golden Hind* he circumnavigated the globe between 1577 and 1580, plundering the Spanish Pacific trade and returning 'very richly fraught with gold, silver, silk, pearls, and precious stones'.

circumnavigation of the globe (1577–80). Alternatively, they turned to colonization, which was justified on many grounds, but particularly to provide bases from which the war on the Spanish Empire could be waged and the search for the North-West passage could be directed. No successful colony was planted in Elizabeth's reign, but it is interesting that the first attempt was made on Newfoundland in 1583, which was now being visited regularly by fleets of English fishermen, who dried their catch on the shores of the island so that it could be successfully brought to the European markets.

The tension between England and Spain culminated in the war from 1585–1604 during which the Spanish Armada was successfully defeated, though the Spanish threat was never ended. One of the causes of increased tension was Philip II's inheritance of the throne of Portugal in 1580, which meant that most of the world came under his control. In 1591, John Lancaster rounded the Cape of Good Hope and showed that English trade with the East Indies was possible. The East India Company was founded to exploit this trade in 1600, and its subsequent increase had a profound effect on the development of the merchant sailing ship. In this way, the basis of English trade for the next 200 years had been laid by the time of Elizabeth's death in 1603, but it was held back by the shortcomings of of English shipping.

16th Century Ships

There was never any great difference between the merchant ship and the man of war until the end of the 17th century. Merchant ships had always needed to be armed against pirates, but when Elizabethan seamen began to sail the oceans in

10 Carracks at Dover. This was the fleet that accompanied Henry VIII on his visit to France to meet King Francis I on the Field of the Cloth of Gold in 1520. The flagship in the centre is probably the *Henry Grace à Dieu*, one of the largest English ships afloat at that time. The beam of a carrack was very wide to cope with the weight of the guns and the tall fore and rear castles added to the cumbersome nature of these ships.

11 John Hawkins (1532–1595) played an important part in the development of the galleon. As Treasurer of the Navy to Queen Elizabeth I, he constructed a fleet of galleons, which were faster and more manoeuvrable than the large carracks. Hawkins also made three attempts to open trade between England and the Spanish Empire between 1562 and 1568.

search of trade or booty, the armament became even more important. The decay of English shipping in the mid-16th century ensured, however, that the details of ship design did change between the reign of Henry VIII (1509–1547) and the reign of Queen Elizabeth (1558–1603). In both reigns the merchant ships were merely smaller versions of the war ships.

Henry VIII built a fleet of large carracks, which were huge, impressive ships of 1,000 tons or more, built for show rather than for service. They had extremely elaborate fore and sterncastles, sometimes four storeys high, which protruded fore and aft over stem and stern of the ship. They also carried a heavy armament of cannon. The *Henry Grace à Dieu,* later rebuilt and renamed the *Great Harry,* had a broadside of guns which protruded through the actual hull at lower deck level. The weight of the guns, which numbered 186 in all, made it essential that the hull should be broad and tub-like, so that the very heavy iron would not topple the ship over. The normal ratio of length of keel to beam (width) in Henry's ships was two to one, whereas in Elizabeth's ships it was three to one. The keel was about two-thirds the length of the ship from stem to stern post, so the length of the keel should never be mistaken for the length of the ship.

Henry's fleet decayed from disuse and lack of maintenance and it was necessary to rebuild a fleet to meet the Spanish danger in the 1570s. John Hawkins, as Treasurer of the Navy, was mainly responsible for the fleet of galleons that helped defeat the Armada. These galleons were much smaller than Henry VIII's carracks;

12 The *Ark Royal,* a galleon built for Sir Walter Raleigh in 1587. It was first called the *Ark Raleigh,* but was renamed the *Ark Royal* when it had been sold to Elizabeth I. It has the typical projecting beak at the bow, and two mizzen masts with three lateen sails. It was highly praised by Lord Howard of Effingham and he used it as his flagship when he commanded the English fleet which defeated the Spanish Armada in 1588.

the prototype was Drake's *Revenge,* which was completed in 1575 and weighed about 500 tons. They were equipped with lighter guns called culverins, but as their brass barrels were cast in a piece and then bored, they were capable of withstanding large charges and they also achieved great accuracy. Elizabethan galleons lost the projecting forecastle and instead had a low projecting beak, with the forecastle set back from the stem. This arrangement was known as the galleon bow. Their great advantage was their manoeuvrability and speed which made them ideal craft for threatening the Spanish treasure routes.

The number of masts increased to four on the larger ships. The addition was the bonaventure mast, which was at the stem and was set with a lateen sail. It acted as a second mizzen, but it had a very short life and had entirely disappeared by 1640. Changes in the structure of the mast also made it possible to increase the sail area. Top sails and top gallant sails had been used on Henry's ships, but as long as the top-masts, to which these sails were attached, were a permanent fixture, they were likely to be damaged in bad weather. Hawkins introduced top-masts which could be easily dismantled, so that extra masts and sails were added with less fear. By 1600, top-masts and top gallant masts, together with their sails, were standard equipment on all the larger warships.

The new merchant ships that were built to carry the new trade incorporated Hawkins's 'long ship' principle, but unless they were particularly large would have a simpler rig. A medium-sized merchant ship would have three masts with top sails on fore and main sail, while even a 20-ton row barge would have three masts. These ships could also be used to fight in war and many of them were used to fight the Armada. Of the merchantmen that fought in 1588, the largest one was 400 tons and the smallest 20 tons. The average tonnage of the 30 ships supplied by the City of London was 150 tons.

England's victory over the Spanish in 1588 was a triumph of the galleon over the Spanish carrack, but it was not the result of any longstanding English seafaring tradition. England's emergence as a world trading nation only began in the 16th century and it was not to be confirmed for another century.

3 The Rise of English Shipping

The Dutch Flyboat

The important consideration in shipping is not the value of a cargo, but its bulk. One or two ships a year returning from the East Indies brought back oriental goods like silks, spices and porcelain, which were worth hundreds of thousands of pounds, while coal or timber of equivalent value might fill a hundred ships. The short regular hauls to the ports of North Eastern Europe were therefore, from a shipping point of view, far more important than the more glamorous trades to the West Indies or India. It was a factor for the government to heed, as it was from the trading ships that seamen were recruited in time of war. The Newcastle coal trade, for instance, was described as 'if not the only, yet the special nursery, and school of seamen'.

The position in these near trades in 1600 was that they were almost wholly carried in foreign ships, usually Dutch. The Dutch seamen, although they were fighting a war of independence against the Spanish which did not finally end until 1648, took the opportunity to take over the role of the Hanseatic League as the bulk carriers of Northern Europe, whether it was corn, timber or coal. In 1593, seven out of eight ships clearing Newcastle with loads of coal for foreign ports

13 Dutch flyboat. This Dutch ship was the type that achieved Dutch commercial supremacy in the early seventeenth century. The port in the background is Rotterdam.

were foreigners, mainly Dutch. A pamphlet of 1615 declared 'Hither even to the mine's mouth come all our Neighbour Country nations with their Ships continually, employing their own shipping and mariners.'

The main reason for Dutch success was their ship called the flyboat or fluit, which was specially designed for cargo work. Whereas English merchant ships were dual purpose, having guns and extensive superstructures to face attack, the Dutch built light, slow ships which had no armament and an unusually high volume of cargo space. As the articles they were carrying were bulky and cheap, the loss of a ship was of no importance. What mattered most was that goods should be carried as cheaply as possible. The greatest saving that the Dutch made was in manpower, as the flyboats carried far less sail than a man of war. A government paper said in 1626, 'The Flemings have eaten us out, by reason that they carry half as cheap again as we can, in regard that their fashioned ships sail with so few men. Whereupon our merchants do usually lade the Flemings and let out own lie still.'

The bulk trades were also important to English shipping, despite this competition. It has been estimated that more than half of English seamen were engaged either in the Newcastle coal trade or in the Newfoundland and Iceland fisheries. The Newfoundland cod fishing reached its peak in the early 17th century when 200 to 300 ships were going there each year, but it declined later when the permanent New England and Newfoundland colonists began to dominate the fishing grounds.

The turning point for English mercantile fortunes occurred during the Interregnum. English traders were given protection from competition by the Navigation Act, which was passed by the Rump of the Long Parliament in 1651 and approved again after Charles II's restoration in 1660. This confined trade with the English colonies to English ships and allowed foreigners to import only their country's own products. It meant that the Dutch could no longer bring in the products of the Baltic to England, though they could still distribute English products to Europe.

This legislation could hardly have been effective, however, if England had not acquired the means to carry her own bulk trade. The necessary shipping was gained during the first Anglo-Dutch war 1652–54, which broke out partly as a result of the Navigation Act. The number of merchant ships of the flyboat type taken from the Dutch during this war was enormous. The tonnage taken in prizes may well have equalled that of the whole existing English merchant fleet. Moreover, the recurrence of the wars against the Dutch enabled the English to replenish their shipping, so that from the middle of the century onwards it had a good balance between armed merchantmen and lighter flyboats.

English Bulk Trades
The expansion of English shipping was based on two commodities—timber and coal. They only accounted for a small proportion of the value of English trade,

14 Newcastle-upon-Tyne, a great coal port from Tudor times onwards. The North-Eastern ports also made a great contribution to the development of English bulk-carrying ships in the eighteenth century.

perhaps two or three per cent, but they accounted for up to 50 per cent of its volume. The captured Dutch ships were used in these trades, but by the end of the 17th century British shipbuilders were beginning to build similar ships themselves.

The ports of the Eastern coast had always taken an active part in coastal shipping, even though their share of the further trades was being lost to London. Ipswich, according to Daniel Defoe, was the greatest town in England for large colliers or coal ships employed between Newcastle and London until the last quarter of the 17th century. The coal trade was a really thriving trade from Queen Elizabeth's reign onwards; the tonnage of coal being shipped along the coast exceeded the whole volume of English imports every year.

The lead in shipbuilding and ship ownership moved from the East coast ports like Ipswich to North-East England at the beginning of the 18th century. It was there that the English equivalent of the Dutch flyboat, called the pink, was built. The term pink referred to the shape of the stern, which was narrow at the top and broader below, to give it more stowing capacity. They were large three-masted ships of around 300 tons suited to the task of carrying masts, timber and any bulky commodity. During the 18th century, places like Whitby and Sunderland were centres of thriving shipbuilding, and to this very day there is a public

25

house overlooking the Thames at the point where the colliers passed called the *Prospect of Whitby*.

London was also a great shipbuilding centre, but it had always been the centre for the great trading companies and therefore concentrated on the strongly-built armed ships for the Levant, East Indies and West Indies trades. London continued to attract trade and population to itself so that there were continual complaints from the outports that London's dominance was causing their decline. The port area was extending down the river past Wapping to Limehouse, and the Great Fire of 1666 seemed to make little difference. In fact, the rebuilding of the City must have given a stimulus to the Baltic trade as the former

15   This Danish timber barque was the type of ship developed by the Dutch in the seventeenth century for carrying bulk cargoes. It is almost square in shape, which proved excellent for its cargo-carrying qualities but made it extremely cumbersome to sail.

oak frame houses were giving way to brick-walled houses with all the inner flooring and framing in softwood, which came from the Baltic.

This was only one reason for the huge increase in the Baltic trade. The English ship-building industry could no longer depend on supplies of English oak and elm, which were becoming scarce, and began to use Baltic oak for the frame (though English oak was still preferred), Baltic softwood—fir, spruce and pine— for decking and planking, and Norwegian pine for masts. The Baltic trade also supplied all the other shipping materials, hemp (for ropes), flax (for sails), pitch and tar (for waterproofing). Cromwell realised the importance of this area when he said in 1658, 'If the Dutch can shut us out of the Baltic Sea and make themselves masters of that, where is your trade? Where are the materials to defend your shipping?'

Most English shipping, therefore, was operating in the vicinity of the British Isles either engaged in the coastal trades or carrying coal to the continent and timber to England. These bulk-carrying ships did not work like a modern tramp ship, moving round the world looking for cargoes. They tended to concentrate on one commodity and one route, though it was known for timber ships to transfer to the seasonal French wine trade from October to January. It was said that all the goods that were exchanged for Baltic timber would have fitted into one ship a year. Even though this is an exaggeration, it does draw attention to the fact that ships had to proceed to the Baltic in ballast or only part loaded.

The Rise of the Western Ports

The most notable phenomenon in the trade of the 18th century was the rise of the Western ports like Liverpool and Bristol. Bristol had been a great port at the end of the Middle Ages, but it had suffered in the 16th century when the products of the west of England, especially Cotswold and Wiltshire broadcloth, were diverted to London. It re-emerged in the 17th century as a centre for cod-fishing and trade with America and the West Indies in sugar and tobacco. Bristol was the second largest port in England until about 1750, when Liverpool took over that position. Liverpool's rapid growth was partly based on sugar and tobacco, partly on the increasing demand for Cheshire rock salt, but primarily on the growth of the slave trade. The western ports in no way detracted from London's importance. It just meant that whereas London had a virtual monopoly of foreign trade from 1500 to 1650, this was no longer the case after 1700.

The trades from the Western Ports were mainly of a triangular nature. The cod, which was caught off Newfoundland, was dried and sold in Portugal, Spain and the Western Mediterranean, whence oil, fruit and wine were taken home in return. The slaves which were purchased in West Africa in exchange for cottons, firearms and trinkets, were taken to the West Indies in exchange for sugar, and sometimes to Virginia in exchange for tobacco. Sugar and tobacco were in great demand in all Europe and became the basis for a thriving re-export trade. It was these tropical products that became an important alternative to cloth in England's continental export markets.

The slave trade, therefore, became an important link in the English trading system. The slave trade began with Hawkins, was developed by the Royal African Company in the 17th century, but became really important after England had been granted the right to sell slaves in the Spanish Empire by the Treaty of Utrecht (1713). Between 1713 and 1733, 150,000 slaves were imported into Spanish and English America, and in the 1740s, there were said to be 55 Liverpool, 40 Bristol and ten London ships annually engaged in the trade.

Slavers tried to leave England in September, so that they could purchase their slaves from the black chieftains and Moorish dealers on the West African coast during the winter. They would then arrive in the West Indies at the end of April for the sugar sales. The aim was then to reach home before the Caribbean hurricanes and the English October storms. Such a programme could not be maintained year after year, so they could be found departing at all times of the year.

The trade was monstrously cruel and degrading to human life. The slaves were packed into the holds and onto shelves, so that they barely had room either to lie down or to stand up. A death rate of one in three during the sea voyage was not uncommon in the 17th century. Survival rates were improved by washing the slaves and by fumigating the ships with tar and brimstone and one slaver at least,

16 This picture shows how slaves were packed on board a slave ship. Fig. 3 shows how the shelves were incorporated. This barbarous slave trade was one of the main reasons behind the rise of Liverpool as a great port in the eighteenth century.

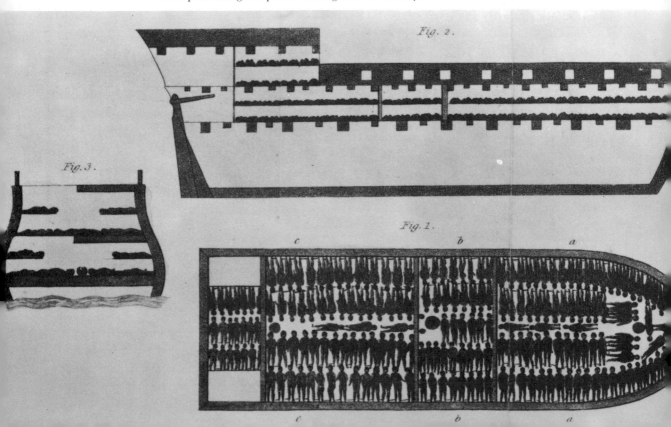

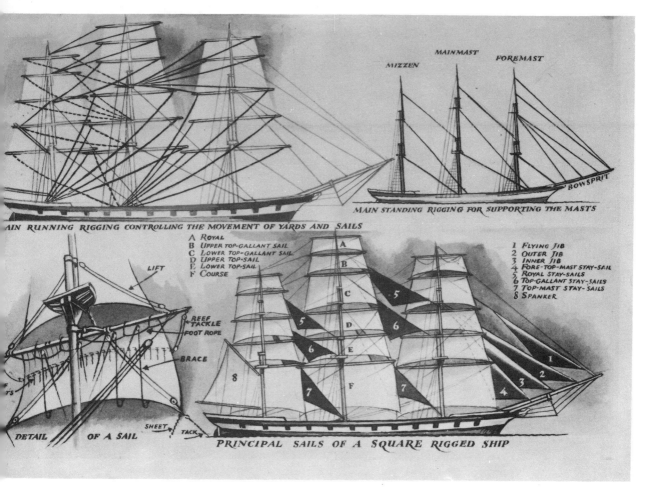

MIZZEN MAINMAST FOREMAST

MAIN STANDING RIGGING FOR SUPPORTING THE MASTS

BOWSPRIT

MAIN RUNNING RIGGING CONTROLLING THE MOVEMENT OF YARDS AND SAILS

A ROYAL
B UPPER TOP-GALLANT SAIL
C LOWER TOP-GALLANT SAIL
D UPPER TOP-SAIL
E LOWER TOP-SAIL
F COURSE

1 FLYING JIB
2 OUTER JIB
3 INNER JIB
4 FORE-TOP-MAST STAY-SAIL
5 ROYAL STAY-SAILS
6 TOP-GALLANT STAY-SAILS
7 TOP-MAST STAY-SAILS
8 SPANKER

LIFT

REEF TACKLE
FOOT ROPE

BRACE

DETAIL OF A SAIL SHEET TACK

PRINCIPAL SAILS OF A SQUARE RIGGED SHIP

17 A fully-rigged ship. The term 'ship' describes a type of vessel with three or more masts rigged with square sails on all masts. In the detail of a sail, the reefing points are small lengths of rope, which made it possible to use only a fraction of the sail if necessary. The rest could be rolled and laced up.

the pious John Newton who later became a priest and an abolitionist, was able to say at the end of his last slave voyage in 1754, 'I had the pleasure of returning thanks in all the churches for our African voyage, performed without any disaster, or the loss of a single man.'

The end of the 18th century was a period of rapid expansion for English shipping. A long and bitter struggle was fought with the French for commercial and colonial supremacy, and won, and a vigorous new trade was being developed with the American colonies, even after they won their independence in 1783 by the Treaty of Versailles. America became the growth market which absorbed the manufactured articles that were being produced in increasing numbers by the improved machinery at the beginning of the Industrial Revolution. Early industrialisation and domination of the oceanic routes were the basis of England's

18 Discharging a collier brig. A brig is a two-masted sailing ship, which is square-rigged on both masts except for the fore and aft spanker. It grew in popularity as a merchant ship and by 1800 was the most common merchant ship. This picture shows the difficulty of unloading a cargo such as coal.

trading supremacy in the 19th century, but it would not have been possible without the growth of shipping.

Changes in Ships 1600-1800

Merchant ships engaged on the further routes continued to be built and armed like men of war, especially the East Indiamen. By the 18th century, the East India Company was building its own ships which were of great size. The normal

East Indiaman was 700 tons and was designed like a naval frigate, while the largest ships of 1,200 tons followed closely the dimensions of a 64-gun man-of-war. Large ships of up to 600 tons were also used in the Baltic trade and the North Russian timber trade, but ships trading with America were usually no more than 400 tons. The West Indiaman was far less like a man-of-war; mainly because it did not have through decks. Its deck was stepped so that there would be more headroom in the forecastle and in the poop.

These large, well-furnished and lavishly-decorated ships were built in London; a less spectacular merchant ship was the northern barque. The word 'barque' came to mean a three-masted vessel, with two square-rigged masts and one fore and aft rigged, but in the mid-18th century it was said of the barque that 'our northern mariners, who are trained in the coal trade, apply this distinction to a broad sterned boat, which carried no ornamental figure on the stern or prow.' It was, therefore, the figurehead on the prow, an elaborate piece of wood carving, and the gilding and decoration of the stern that differentiated the far-ranging company ship from the collier. The colliers were perfectly safe ocean-going vessels, and were employed by Captain James Cook on all three of his voyages of discovery

19 A schooner is also distinguished by its rigging. The two square sails on the main mast were quite common on British schooners, though not on American. This schooner, the *Dispatch*, was built in Scotland in 1888.

20 The ketch was a two-masted vessel with a tall main mast and a small mizzen. After 1870 the ketch became popular as a rig for small commercial craft. This British ketch was built in Dorset in 1876.

between 1768 and 1780. Although they were barques, Cook employed ship-rigging by putting square sails on the mizzen mast. These vessels were built for cargo carrying and therefore had a wide, squat hull, which gave the maximum space inside.

Until the end of the 18th century, it was the shape of the hull that normally classified the ship. The colliers that Cook used were also called cats, after their cat-built hulls, while the pink was named after the stern shape. In the 19th century, however, it became the practice to classify the vessel by the rigging and the number of masts.

Most of the improvement in ships occurred in the rigging. By 1800, the three-masted ship had supplied herself with six times as much sail as had been used by the Portuguese caravel 300 years before. Much of the extra sail was only suitable for fair weather sailing in light winds. A great step forward was taken in the sail plan of the naval ship the *Royal Sovereign*, built in 1637, which had royal sails as a fourth tier of sail on the main and fore masts. These extra sails gradually came into general use on merchant ships, although the royal was not adopted until 150 years afterwards. Studding sails were also introduced early in the 17th century and became quite widely used. These sails were spread or extensions to the main sail and top-sail booms of the fore and main masts and increased the ship's sail area considerably.

Other additional sails improved the ship's capacity to make progress against a headwind. They were particularly valuable in enabling ships to beat their way down the English Channel against the prevailing north-westerly winds. The most important new sail was the jib, which was a triangular sail spread between an extension to the bowsprit called the jib-boom and the fore mast. It had been used on one-mast ships since the 16th century, but wasn't used on merchant ships until the 1720s. In 1794, a second jib called a flying jib was introduced. The other sails which help the ship to tack were the stay sails, which were also triangular and were spread on the stays (support ropes) which held the masts in position. The typical ship of 1750 would carry two staysails and many carried three.

The lateen sail changed shape during this period and became the spanker. By about 1780, the long lateen yard had been replaced by a shorter yard called a spanker gaff, which was held out at an angle from the mizzen mast and made it possible for the spanker to be used as a yacht-like sail in fair winds.

By the end of the 18th century, the brig was beginning to replace the ships and barques as the commonest vessel. Among the smaller vessels of under 200 tons, the two-masted brig came to predominate. It had all the characteristics of a ship except that the main-mast was absent. This kind of vessel by 1800 was carrying most of the trade with Southern Europe, Germany and Holland, as well as much of the transatlantic trade. It was mainly used for carrying coal and it became known as the collier brig.

There had therefore been no great change in the basic parts of the ship for three centuries, but the sailing ship had been perfected so that it could fulfil every activity, from war to bulk trading, efficiently. There was also an increasing specialisation in ships so that they could fulfil their functions better. The 19th century, however, brought a new form of power which was to subject the sailing ship to real competition.

Development of the Sailing Ship

Period	Ship	Developments

Period

21 800–1100
(Viking
Longboat)

Ship

Developments

Steering board
Double ended
Single square sail
Clinker built
Oars

22 1100–1400
(Seal from
Poole)

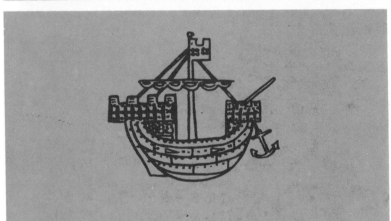

Forecastle and Sternc[a]
become part of the shi[p]
Bowsprit
No oars
Stern rudder
Crows nest

23 1400–1500
(English ship)
1485

Three masts
Lateen sail on mizze[n]
Sprit sail
Clinker built

34

Period	Ship	Developments

24 1500–1600
(Galleon
c. 1600)

Extra mast making four
Top-sails and top gallant
sails
Broad in beam
Gun ports in hull
Carvel built

25 1600–1800
(French ship
c. 1800)

Through decks
Lateen turns into spanker
Jib and stay sails (for
tacking)
Royal and studding sails
(for driving)
Three rows of guns

26 1800–1900
(*Dashing Wave*
clipper ship)

Extra storeys of sail
(skysails)
Lengthened hull
Narrower beam
Composite hull

35

4   Steam Versus Sail

The Advent of Steam

Steam power played a big part in quickening industrial production at the end of the 18th century. It powered the pumping engine which enabled miners to mine deeper; in 1781, James Watt patented a rotary motion engine which could drive the new textile machines, and very soon the same kind of engine was used to drive paddle wheels on board ships. The first practicable steamship was the *Charlotte Dundas,* built by William Symington and tested on the Forth-Clyde Canal. In 1803, it travelled for 19 miles along this canal at six miles an hour and showed possibilities as a river craft. The first steam-powered British vessel to venture out to sea was Henry Bell's *Comet* of 1812, which plied as a passenger vessel in the Clyde estuary in Scotland. Within the next 20 years they were commonly used for coastal passenger services and as pleasure boats in estuaries.

The early steamships had extremely inefficient engines. They were all paddle steamers until the invention of the screw as a means of propulsion in 1838. The paddles were cumbersome attachments at all times, but they also had to be adjusted according to the depth of the ship in the water. The steamers were, relative to their size, very heavy in coal consumption and much of the space was taken up by coal bunkers. There was, therefore, little space for cargo, so the early successful steamship services concentrated on carrying passengers and mail. A technical difficulty was that as the coal was consumed, the ship began to lift out of the water and it was therefore necessary to increase the diameter of the paddles.

The Atlantic was an ideal testing ground for the steamship as it could just be covered without the need to take on more coal. The early steamship crossings were made by ships that used a mixture of steam and sail. The first steamship to cross the Atlantic was the American vessel *Savannah,* which crossed from New York to Liverpool in 1819, but it only used its steam engines for 85 hours on a 25 day voyage. The Dutch ship *Curaçao,* in 1825, and the Canadian ship *Royal William,* in 1833, both crossed the ocean under steam power, but both had to stop the engines from time to time to clear the boilers of salt.

The voyages which led people to believe that regular steamship services were really possible were those of the *Sirius* and the *Great Western* in 1838. They had a race to New York as part of the competition of two groups of businessmen to win the government's mail contract. The adventures of the *Sirius,* which was not built for Atlantic service and was only purchased by the Bristol and American Navigation Company after it had been found impossible to build a new ship, illustrate all the difficulties of the route. She was the first ship to cross the Atlantic on steam power alone, but she only managed it by chopping up the ship's furniture to use

27 The *Sirius* (above) and the *Great Western* (below). These two ships took part in the famous race in 1838, which showed that ships could cross the Atlantic on steam alone. The *Sirius* arrived in New York first, but the *Great Western*, starting later, took three days less. The *Great Western* was designed by Isambard Kingdom Brunel.

in the boilers after the coal was finished, and by taking on coal at New York's pilot station for the last few miles into harbour. The *Great Western* was a few hours behind, having started from England later, and covered the journey in 15 days five hours, three days faster than the *Sirius*.

The *Great Western* was a symbolic ship, as it was designed by Isambard Brunel who saw it as a means by which his great new railway from London to Bristol, the Great Western Railway, could be extended to New York. The remaining question after the successful voyage was whether the greater regularity and speed of the steamship would compensate for the extra cost. It was clear that the fares of the 94 passengers on board the *Great Western* could not make the route profitable. Everything depended on the mail contract, as letters took up very little room and the government grant was generous. To the fury of the Great Western Syndicate, the contract was given to a Canadian called Samuel Cunard (1838).

Nineteenth-Century Sailing Ships

The route to the East was far less suitable for steamships due to the need for rebunkering. A ship called the *Enterprise* showed what was possible in 1825 by using steam power on a voyage from Falmouth to Calcutta which lasted for 113 days, 64 of them under steam, but there was no follow up.

The most striking change in Eastern trade was the ending of the East India Company's monopoly of trade to India in 1813, and of trade to China in 1833. It led to the disappearance of the East Indiaman from the sea. They were not commercial vessels and had only been continued due to the tradition of heavy armament on this route, and the conservatism of the Company. They were replaced by faster Blackwall frigates, built in London, which had flushdecks without any raised poop and a greater length in proportion to their breadth. The ratio of breadth to length on the East Indiamen had been 1 to 4; on the Blackwall frigates it reached 1 to 4.7.

The most efficient sailing ships were produced by the Americans. Their fast clippers gained a good reputation during the Napoleonic Wars in Europe, when they began to carry European goods as neutral ships. When the war was over, a regular monthly service was offered from New York to Liverpool, entirely operated in the fast clippers. They lengthened the hulls until they were $5\frac{1}{2}$ times the beam and they increased their tonnage to 1,800 tons. As the design improved, they could cross the Atlantic from East to West in less than 14 days and from West to East in under 18 days. They benefited from the increased emigration from Europe to America, which, by 1835, amounted to around 50,000 people a year, and for the moment they faced no competition from steamships as cargo carriers.

It was the discovery of gold in 1851 at Bendigo and Ballarat, in Victoria, Australia, which stimulated English shippers to make use of clippers. There was a great emigration to Australia, which was carried partly by Blackwall frigates from the China route and partly by the British Black Ball Line, who purchased second-hand a whole fleet of American Atlantic clippers for the purpose. These were later supplemented by some new clippers to the design of the best American designer, Donald MacKay. These clippers were given the mail contract and they guaranteed a delivery in 68 days.

The success of the clippers on this route led to the development of the last profitable cargo sailing ships—the tea clippers and the wool clippers. In the tea clippers, the length was still further increased until it was almost six times the beam. Well-known ships such as *Thermopylae* and *Cutty Sark* were built, in 1868 and 1869 respectively, for speed, so that their shippers could be first in the home market with the new season's tea. As tea clippers their life was particularly short, for the opening of the Suez Canal in 1869 gave the steamships the benefit of a shorter route, which the sailing ships did not use.

28 Emigration to America and Australia gave a great boost to shipping in the nineteenth century. This drawing of emigrants at dinner shows what it was like below deck. The sleeping bunks can be seen on each side of the tables.

29 The famous tea clipper *Cutty Sark*, built in 1869. It now stands at Greenwich in dry dock and is open to the public. The tea clippers were 'composites', which means that the frame of the ship was iron, but the hull walls of wood. The *Cutty Sark* did most of its work on the wool route to Australia.

The tea clippers were therefore transferred to the Australia route, where sailing ships could achieve remarkable speeds. They made use of the south east trade winds in the South Atlantic and then sailed close to the Antarctic so that they could make use of the westerlies of the Southern Hemisphere. After leaving Australia they would proceed with the westerlies to Cape Horn and thus complete a circumnavigation of the globe. The wool clippers were built with more width to cope with their more bulky cargo. In order to maintain the yacht-like qualities of a clipper, the length was increased to over six times the width and the size increased to 2,000 tons. In this way, the sailing clippers continued to be competitive until 1890. There was never anything wrong with their speed; it was merely that to reach these speeds captains had to take risks and the passengers were subjected to discomforts. The decks were continually awash and the passengers were battened down in the suffocating atmosphere below.

Packets and Passengers

The American sailing clippers dominated the Atlantic routes until about 1860 when the steam engine was made more efficient. The most important invention was John Elder's compound engine in 1854, which made much more efficient use of the available steam and thus used less coal. With the older engines, anything up to three quarters of the weight carrying capacity of the steamship was taken up by coal, and therefore little room was left for cargo. The Americans were so certain that the steamship would never be able to compete with the sailing ship that they gave next to no encouragement to their steamship owners. The only advantage that steamships could offer was their ability to keep to schedule. At their best, sailing ships were faster, but if the winds were not right they could be considerably delayed. This delay did not matter for cargo, nor did it matter to many immigrants to America who just wanted a cheap passage, but it did matter to the British government who wanted their letters delivered on time.

It was the government mail contracts which put British steam shipping firms onto their feet. Shipping companies used steamships for normal duties as early as 1826, when the General Steam Navigation Company put them onto the London-Portugal route. The first regular steam service, however, was that offered by Willcox and Anderson, which left for Portugal and Spain every fortnight. It ran at a loss for two years, but in 1837 was saved by the government mail contract which was worth £29,600 each year. In 1840, they also won the contract to carry mail to Alexandria in Egypt, whence it was carried by the East India Company to the Orient (the East). In the same year they were given a charter as the Peninsular and Oriental Navigation Company (P & O).

There was great competition for the transatlantic mail contract, but it was finally won by Samuel Cunard. The Cunard Line was established in 1840 with a fleet of four steamships and depended completely on the mail contract, which was worth £2,300 on each voyage, for its profitability. There was also a very great

30 Samuel Cunard (1787–1865). Although he was born in Canada, Cunard became the founder of a great British shipping company and the first regular Atlantic steamship line. Cunard entered into a contract with the British government in 1839 for the conveyance of the mails between Liverpool and Halifax (Nova Scotia), Boston and Quebec. The first voyage of Cunard's line was made by the *Britannia* in 1840.

demand for passenger services to America which helped to keep the steamships full. Between 1845 and 1855, 2½ million people sailed from Great Britain to North America, which kept all kinds of ships busy, whether steam or sail. With the success of the first companies, it was open to other groups of business men to start steam packet services to other areas of the world. Some were successful, like the Pacific Steam Navigation Company, some less so, like the Royal Mail Steam Packet Company service to the West Indies.

The shortcomings of the early steamships are illustrated by the fortunes of the *Great Eastern*, which was started in 1854 by Isambard Brunel for the Indian and Australian route. Brunel's hope was that if only a steamship were built large enough, the weakness of having too little cargo space would be offset. He therefore planned a ship of 19,000 tons, which was five or six times the size of any then in use. It incorporated the most recent improvements, namely a completely iron hull and screw (propeller) propulsion, though it also had paddles and facilities for sails. This enormous vessel, which could carry 2,000 passengers and 6,000 tons of cargo, was fated from the start. The ship was not successfully launched until three months after the first attempt, and she was never fast enough to be a commercial success either as a cargo or passenger steamer. She did her best work in laying the transatlantic cable.

The Triumph of Steam

By 1870, the steamship was beginning to supersede the sailing ship. The eventual supremacy of steam was based on three improvements, the compound engine, the screw propeller and the iron hull.

The compound engine was steadily improved so that the same steam was used to drive first two, then three and even four pistons. Fuel consumption had been reduced by half by 1872, and the saved space could be used for cargo. The screw propeller was used for some time in addition to paddles, so that there was no immediate increase in efficiency. Its advantage was that it was fully submerged

31 The *Great Eastern*. This ill-fated ship was designed by Isambard Kingdom Brunel on a grand scale. It was much larger than any ship previously attempted and although started in 1854, it still mixed sail with steam and screw propulsion with paddle propulsion.

and was therefore continuously efficient, whereas the paddle was only partly submerged. It was also capable of rapid and smooth rotation, which made it possible to introduce fast running engines which were more compact and saved space. Transatlantic steamers driven by single screw propulsion only began to appear in 1865, and in 1888 the twin-screw principle made possible a great improvement in power.

The other great improvement was the introduction of the iron hull. In sailing ships the wooden hull had a long life. The tea clippers were 'composites', that is, wooden walls on an iron frame. On steamers, however, the iron hull was accepted as being lighter and more efficient as early as the 1840s, and came in decisively with the use of the screw propeller. The *Great Britain*, completed in 1843, was the first iron ship and the first screw-propelled ship to cross the Atlantic, and thereafter most steamships were iron. The use of iron and later steel made it possible to build much larger ships, which again opened up new space for cargo.

Although British shipyards were producing more steamers than sailing ships by 1865, the sailing ship still dominated English merchant shipping. In 1870, there were 4,580,000 tons of sailing ships on the British Register of Shipping, compared with 901,000 tons of steamships. From that time on, however, while the tonnage of sail contracted, the tonnage of steam increased.

The triumph of the steamer over the clipper also marked the triumph of English shipping over American. The Americans had held the advantage in cargo carrying on the transatlantic route since the Napoleonic wars, but this declined with the clipper. No government had given so much encouragement to the steamship lines as the British government, so that British shipyards and shipping companies had

32 The *Great Britain* returns home. Launched in 1843 in Bristol, the *Great Britain* was abandoned as a hulk in the Falkland Islands in 1866, when she was demasted while rounding Cape Horn, but in 1970 she was salvaged and towed home on a pontoon to be restored and used as a museum. She was the first ocean-going ship with an iron hull and the first screw-propelled ship to cross the Atlantic.

33 This advertisement for the Cunard line shows the change in Atlantic steamships between 1840 and 1893. The Britannia was the first Cunard ship. All the early steamers were paddle steamers like this and all of them carried sail as an alternative means of propulsion. The *Campania* was a typical ocean liner of the late nineteenth century.

a long lead in steam shipping, when the advantages of steam became clear. The first important European Company, the Nord Deutscher Lloyd, was founded in 1857, well after its English counterparts, and even then they bought British ships.

Lloyds and the Baltic

Two very important services to shipping developed in the seventeenth and eighteenth centuries from coffee houses. Lloyds, which is still the greatest marine insurance institution in the world, grew from Lloyds Coffee House in Tower Street, London. The Baltic is the freight market in the city, where shippers sell their cargo space. This too started in a coffee house, which eventually became known as the Virginia and Baltic Coffee House. It was the habit of the shipping interest to frequent these coffee houses and then enterprising proprietors began to give them extra services.

Mr. Lloyd provided his customers with a news-sheet called 'Lloyd's News', since renamed 'Lloyd's List', and his establishment rapidly became a recognised centre for marine insurance. Here, in return for premiums, underwriters accepted

45

risks, in whole or in part, so that individual owners could obtain adequate insurance cover for their ships and no single underwriter had, necessarily, to bear the entire risk.

Lloyds is now situated in Lime Street, in the city of London, and in the vast Underwriting Room, underwriters still insure ships and cargoes. They also accept non-marine, aviation and motor business offered to them by brokers and their whole annual premium income is now well in excess of £600 m. Much of the tradition of the coffee house is still maintained; the messengers, for instance, are still called waiters and the boxes at which the underwriters sit are like the coffee house seats. A more recent tradition is that of the Lutine Bell, taken from a ship that sank in 1799, which is rung once for bad news, such as the loss of an overdue vessel, and twice for good news.

The Baltic is a club where brokers handle freight and cargo space instead of insurance. It provides a place where merchants and shipowners can match their requirements. Such a centre became much more necessary after the invention of telegraph, which made it possible to make sure that your ship never travelled empty. Brokers became knowledgeable in certain trades so that if a ship was needed to carry 10,000 tons of tin ore for 'first half December loading' at Singapore, they will know who to ask in the Baltic. Freight rates will also be fixed and the business is done. There are set forms for sealing contracts. The contract made between the shipowner's broker and the shipper is set out in a document called a 'charter party'.

Lloyds and the Baltic therefore play an essential part in the successful management of trade. Both handle a good deal of the shipping business of the world. They won reputations for efficiency at the time when British ships were beginning to dominate world trade and have never lost it. Both handle other business than shipping, but their main connection is still with trade.

34 This caricature of 1798 shows the Subscribers' Room at Lloyds Coffee House in the Royal Exchange. Mr Lloyd, the proprietor, encouraged people seeking insurance to come here and Lloyds became the greatest marine insurance institute in the world.

5   Shipping Supremacy

Free Trade

The years from 1870 to 1914 mark the high-point of British shipping supremacy. During this period Great Britain possessed half of the world's shipping and carried half of the world's trade. In 1870, her command of world trade was unchallenged, but as the years went by, other countries in Europe industrialized, the great wealth of the United States began to be exploited and even Asian countries like Japan were challenging British control of some markets. It was clear by 1914, that the British share of world trade was bound to decline and that an era had ended.

The government policy during these years was one of free trade. This meant that Great Britain did not tax foreign trade at the ports. Customs duties had been levied in the past partly as a source of government income and partly as a means of discouraging the import of foreign goods. The introduction of income tax as a direct tax on people's wealth made them unnecessary as a source of government income and Great Britain's lead over the rest of the world in the production of manufactured goods dispelled all fear of foreign competition. British industry, moreover, needed foreign raw materials, like American cotton or Australian wool, to make their machine-made products, and wanted them to come into the country as easily as possible.

Another aspect of free trade was the old colonial system based on the Navigation Act (1660), which reserved colonial trade for British ships. The argument for keeping this system was a naval and not a commercial one. Trade was a training ground for sailors for the fleet and therefore should be reserved. Even the first great exponent of free trade, a Scotsman called Adam Smith, recognised this argument in his book the 'Wealth of Nations' (1776). 'As defence is of much more importance than opulence, the act of navigation is, perhaps, the wisest of all the commercial regulations of England.'

Adam Smith, as a free trader, would have considered that the law hindered trade, but for a justifiable reason. In 1849, the growing movement for free trade secured the repeal of the Navigation Law as a help to trade. From that time on, English trade prospered and English shipping improved, but it is impossible to know how far the ending of the old colonial system contributed towards this. Against the Navigation Acts, it is sometimes argued that they protected British shipping from foreign competition and therefore deprived the shipping industry of any stimulus to improve. There are many reports that the officers of British merchant ships were badly disciplined and ill trained in the arts of navigation. It is also clear that the British merchant fleet increased in size only very slowly

47

between 1815–40. In defence of the Navigation Acts, it is said that they secured for British shipping a control of the long-haul imperial routes to India, Australia and America, which became the real basis of the country's shipping tradition.

Standards of discipline and training did improve in British merchant ships after 1850, but this can be attributed to an Act of 1850 'for improving the condition of Masters, Mates and Seamen and maintaining discipline in the Merchant Service'. This gave the Board of Trade supervision of training so that masters and mates had to pass examinations before they gained a certificate; it also laid down minimum standards for seamen's food and accommodation as well as punishments for indiscipline.

Great Britain certainly did maintain a very tight hold over the long ocean routes throughout the century, but this was not all due to the Navigation Act. The great expanding trade in the eighteenth century was that with America, so that by 1800 that continent was absorbing over half of Britain's exports. This happened despite the American War of Independence (1776–1783) and the departure of the United States from the colonial system. The continued expansion of the trade after the Napoleonic War (1793–1815) seems to suggest that the Navigation Act had never been an important factor. This conclusion is important as it means that the British merchant interest should not become over-concerned when young powers nurture their shipping by reserving their own trade to their own ships. It may do them more harm than good.

35   This is the steamship *Anglo-Colombian*, a general cargo ship, arriving in London in 1935 carrying timber and cereals from Vancouver, British Columbia. It has completed a typical unspectacular voyage which is the basic element of Britain's world shipping.

Liners and Tramps

English supremacy can be better explained by her lead in steam shipping and her early industrialization. In the field of shipping, she was very well served by her liner companies, which quickly established a reputation for technical and commercial efficiency and completely transformed the reputation for laxness, which British masters had won in the early 19th century. Many of the liner companies were descended from the old packet lines and clipper firms. The more casual owners in British shipping, like those who owned one ship to carry their own goods, or to hire out for single journeys, gave way to the regular services offered by bigger companies. These companies developed a tradition of ploughing back their profits into the company to provide more modern ships, so that the reputation of the liners remained sound.

The liner referred to here is the cargo liner. It is a specially designed ship, which is planned to cope with the needs of the route which it will serve. It is not designed for carrying bulk cargoes, but is divided up into holds so that a large variety of goods can be successfully handled. It is built to carry all the valuable cargo going to one particular port or country and it normally operates on the longer routes. Britain's domination of the oceanic route was based on these cargo liners, which were the pride of the shipping companies which operated them. Once established, liner routes were very difficult to compete against, first because a very complex organisation was needed on shore to accumulate a cargo for a particular ship, and secondly because every cargo ship is different, as it is tailor-made for the needs of a particular route and therefore not all ships would be suitable for the same job.

British domination of the ocean routes, therefore, was very long-lived. British ships had to carry an increasingly large amount of foreign trade in order to

36 A tramp steamer, the *Asia,* in the Suez Canal in 1887. It is the type of ship that would tramp round the world seeking cargoes.

maintain their share of world trade. When other European countries and America began to produce their own manufactured goods, the British share of total world production dropped, yet British ships were still carrying 52 per cent of world trade in 1912, much of it foreign. British ships carried almost all the trade between the United Kingdom and the Empire, but on top of this they carried much trade for other countries as well.

The position had changed, however, from the 17th century when British shipping grew due to bulk trading in coal and timber. By 1914, British shipping was still thriving, but now it was mainly because she carried most of the world's valuable cargoes. In the carriage of bulk cargoes, she was beginning to lose ground to new shipping nations which developed tramp steamer fleets of their own.

The tramp steamer was a standard bulk carrier, which was purchased ready-made as an all purpose ship that could carry anything from coal to corn. Great Britain had a tremendous advantage in this field, as she had a bulk commodity in the form of coal which had to be carried all round the world to supply the coal bunkering stations on which all shipping depended. Even when foreign countries developed coal industries of their own, there was still a demand for Welsh coal because of its heat-producing qualities. Equally, there were bulk commodities that were needed in England, like corn and sugar, which could be carried back on the return journey.

The tramp steamer, however, did not expect to make a return trip to the home country immediately. Its name is derived from its habit of steaming from port to port as a universal carrier. It was a great advantage if the country of origin had a vigorous trade so that the crews could return to base every now and again, and this, of course, Great Britain had. Effective tramping was made possible by the telegraph, because only then could schedules of work be drawn up for the steamers. Before telegraph, they had to go from port to port in hope of work; after telegraph they could be given prior warning of where their services were needed. The transatlantic cable was laid by the *Great Eastern* in 1866, and thereafter cables were gradually laid round the world, until by 1887, 100,000 miles of cable had been laid. It increased the efficiency of shipping enormously by ensuring that ships were always moving towards the right place at the right time.

On the tramp steamers it was very important to keep wage costs down, as they formed a large proportion of shipping costs. By the 20th century British labour was becoming expensive by world standards, so that British tramps lost their competitive edge. The disadvantage was partly overcome by employing Asiatic crews, who made up one-third of the labour force on British ships in 1903. Nevertheless, countries like Norway and Greece could offer lower rates than British ships at this time because they had lower wage bills. For this reason, Britain's lead in tramp shipping was being challenged especially on the shorter European routes. In 1910, tramp shipping still made up about half of our mercantile marine, so its decline must not be exaggerated.

37 A scene on maindeck. This picture gives a good idea of life on board ship in the early nineteenth century. The ship is carrying armaments and a number of passengers.

Nature of Trade

During the 19th century, the function of British trade changed. In the 18th century, trade was not necessary to the nation's existence and much of it was in commodities which were no more than luxuries. In the 19th century trade became essential.

Its first essential importance was that it supplied British industry with its raw materials. American cotton was so important to Lancashire that the whole county suffered when trade was disrupted by the American Civil War. Australian wool became very important to the woollen industry, and Swedish iron ore was always important to the steel industry due to its high quality.

Later in the century trade was even more vital when Britain became dependent on foreign supplies of food to feed its growing population. The British farmer could compete against the American prairie farmer until about 1870, when the building of the American railways, the improvement of steam shipping and the introduction of the combine-harvester onto the vast open lands, together made it possible to bring American corn into England at a price well below that of British-grown corn. The position was made even worse for the British farmer by the completion of the Canadian Pacific Railway in 1886, which opened up the Canadian prairies.

Farmers, who resorted to pasturing animals as an alternative, were subjected to the competition of New Zealand butter and mutton and Argentine beef after the *Dunedin* had docked in London in 1882 with a cargo of refrigerated meat.

51

38   This picture shows a refrigerated hold and a cargo of meat on board the *New Zealand Star* in 1947.

From this time on, much of the meat consumed in Great Britain came from abroad.

Great Britain had been a regular importer of cereals since 1800, but until 1870 agriculture remained the most important industry. Thereafter, a great depression set in, mainly due to foreign competition, which forced many farmers off the land and caused British agriculture to contract. From this time, the country came to depend on foreign food to feed the growing populations of the British towns.

Britain's trading prosperity in the 19th century was based on the export of cotton and woollen cloth. From 1830 to 1880, these textiles made up 60 per cent of our export trade. Cotton was the more important of the two and thus the long period in which woollen cloth had been Britain's staple export came to an end. Coal was another important export. The coal fields in the British Isles are so near to the sea that freight charges were kept to the minimum.

By 1914, the pattern of British trade was changing yet again, because English cottons were losing their advantage in world markets. European countries began to develop textile industries of their own and governments introduced policies of protection to keep out foreign goods from their home market. Protection is the opposite of free trade. It involves the imposition of high tariffs on goods coming into the country, so that they would be made dearer than home-produced goods. Germany introduced high tariffs in 1879 and many European countries followed suit. Even Canada and Australia adopted high tariff policies.

Great Britain, therefore, had to export new types of goods like machines, engines and ships to keep up her trade, but this meant, of course, that she was giving other countries the wherewithal to produce their own goods and carry their own trade in the future. By the 20th century, both the United States and Germany had surpassed Great Britain as industrial countries and Britain's era of supremacy had ended on the industrial front.

Improvements in Shipping

There was a great advance in the field of safety during this period. The steamship was very much safer than the sailing ship anyway, but seamen benefited also by the accurate charting and surveying of the seas and the provision of light-ships and light-houses. The corporation of Trinity House, which dates from the reign of Henry VIII, had been responsible for lighthouses since 1680, but they now greatly increased their number.

Moreover, throughout the period, Parliament was actively interested in the improvement of conditions in the mercantile marine. The credit for the changes has been given to Samuel Plimsoll, who drew attention to the overloading of ships. Some owners were in the habit of sending out their ships overloaded and in poor condition, but heavily insured. They did not care whether the ship returned or not. They made their profit either way. The Merchant Shipping Act (1876) made a load-line on the side of the ship compulsory and empowered the Board of Trade to stop an overloaded ship leaving port, but still left room for abuse, by allowing the owner to fix where the load-line should be painted. In 1890, however, the Board of Trade took responsibility for fixing the load-line also.

39 Wolf Rock Lighthouse, situated on a rock between Lands End and the Scilly Isles. Light-houses and light-ships are vital for the safety of shipping and are directed by the corporation of Trinity House.

40 This cargo liner, the *Parthia*, was completed in 1963 to ply the Atlantic route for the Cunard Steamship Company. The Plimsoll line can be seen clearly, which means that the holds must be comparatively empty. The gear above the deck is made up of sansom posts and derricks which are here lying flat. All the deck can be removed to give access to the holds. A few passengers could be carried in the stern of the ship.

There was a continual improvement in the size and speed of ships. This can be most clearly demonstrated by listing the size and power of the prestige passenger ships on the Atlantic route.

Launch Year	Vessel	Length Feet	Beam Feet	Tonnage	H.P.	Nationality of Origin
1840	*Britannia*	207	34	1,139	440	British
1858	*Great Eastern*	680	82	18,915	4,890	British
1861	*Scotia*	379	47	3,871	975	British
1874	*Britannia*	455	45	5,004	4,970	British
1881	*City of Rome*	560	52	8,141	11,890	British
1897	*Kaiser Wilhelm der Grosse*	684	72	14,349	31,000	German
1907	*Mauretania*	762	88	31,938	68,000	British
1914	*Majestic*	954	100	56,621	80,000	German
1928	*Bremen*	899	102	51,656	95,000	German
1932	*Normandie*	1,029	118	83,423	160,000	French
1938	*Queen Elizabeth*	1,031	119	83,673	200,000	British
1952	*United States*	990	102	53,329	155,000	American
1967	*Queen Elizabeth 2*	963	105	58,000	120,000	British

It was in ships' engines that there were the greatest changes. The compound engine was improved into the triple and quadruple expansion engines, but the most exciting development was the turbine of Sir Charles Parsons, which was first successfully used on a ship in 1894. Over the next ten years, its use was gradually extended to estuary and channel craft, until it was felt to be suitable for ocean vessels. Its superiority as far as speed was concerned was proved when the *Mauretania*, having been launched in 1906, won back the Blue Riband from Germany and held it for the next 22 years. The Blue Riband is an award given to the fastest passenger ship on the Atlantic route. It was always held by Britain until the German ship *Kaiser Wilhelm der Grosse* won it in 1897.

The great advantage of the turbine was that it drove the main shaft directly and not at second-hand, like the compound engine; it also eliminated all vibration. Its disadvantage at first was that it was very extravagant on fuel at low speeds, but this was put right in 1911 by an improvement which enabled the fast running turbine to be geared down to a more efficient propeller speed for slow running.

The age of coal was giving way to the age of oil. Very few ships were fuelled with oil before 1914, but it began to be favoured after the First World War. It was

41 This drawing shows conditions in the stoke-hole in 1870. Coal was not an easy fuel to use on board ship. Not only was it extremely bulky to carry, but also the coal fires needed regular attention from the stokers.

easier to carry, took up less space and was easier to take on board. It saved the labour of stokers and was slightly more economic. When the *Mauretania* was converted to oil in 1921, the bunker space needed was reduced from 7,000 tons for coal to 5,350 tons for oil, and the engine staff was reduced from 446 to 176. Diesel engines, working on the same principle as lorry engines, were first used in 1912 and were generally accepted as a suitable engine for smaller ships, although the bigger ships used the geared turbine.

The improvements in the steam engine were accompanied by large rises in boiler pressure and dramatic increases in efficiency. This diagram summarizes these facts.

Period	Improvements in construction	Approximate Boiler Pressure lb per sq. inch	Approximate poundage of coal per horse-power
1820–45	paddle wheels	1–10	6.25 to 4.5
1845–50	iron hull	10–20	4.5 to 3.5
1850–65	screw propulsion	20–35	3.5 to 2.9
1865–75	compound engine	35–60	2.9 to 2.2
1875–85	steel hull triple expansion engine	60–125	2.2 to 1.9
1885–1900	twin screws quadruple expansion engine	125–200	1.9 to 1.3
1900–10	turbine engines	195–200	1.3 to 0.683
1911–69	geared turbines	200–350	0.683

6 War and Slump

The First World War

The 1914–18 war had a more extensive effect on the shipping industry than on any other branch of British industrial life. There were few bombs dropped on English towns and factories, but there was a whole-hearted effort by Germany to win the war by depriving Great Britain of her trade. Shipbuilding came nowhere near to replacing the ships lost and in consequence there was a significant reduction in the size of the shipping stock. Great Britain entered the war with 19.26 million tons of sail and steam shipping of over 100 tons (39.4 per cent of the world total), and by 1919 this figure had been reduced to 16.56 million tons (32.5 per cent of the world total).

To provide the needs of British trade, the government had to take ships into temporary control from the beginning. This is called requisitioning or chartering. In 1915, they requisitioned all ships with refrigerated space, which accounted for a quarter of British merchant ships, but by 1917 almost all ships were under charter in this way. It meant that British shipowners could not make large profits out of the constant demand for shipping and the constant danger to which these ships were subjected.

The German menace came from the U-boats, which lurked off the coast of Ireland, to pick off the ships as they approached the home shipping lanes. Luckily,

42   The German U-boat U.35 running on the surface in the Mediterranean and about to submerge. This photograph was taken in May 1917.

43 The British convoy sloop *Coreopsis*, which acted as a Q-boat in the First World War. She disguised herself as a cargo liner hoping to lure the U-boat to the surface.

Admiral von Tirpitz was rather hasty in inaugurating his U-boat campaign when he started in 1915 with only about 25 of them. If he had delayed his attack until 1917 when he had over 200 submarines in service, and surprised the Ministry of Shipping before it had taken adequate countermeasures, the effect could well have been decisive. As it was, the forewarning in 1915 enabled the government to be better prepared in 1917.

The U-boat had weaknesses of its own. It was a swift surface vessel, driven by powerful oil engines at 17 knots, but when it was submerged it had to rely on accumulators, which had a very short life when used for speed, but allowed it to remain under the water for 20 hours at more economical speeds. The accumulators could only be recharged from the oil engines, while on the surface. This meant that it was difficult for U-boats to escape once seen and once listening devices called hydrophones had been invented.

U-boats were armed with from 8 to 20 torpedoes, which provided only a limited strike because a number would miss. They normally surfaced, therefore, to shell the ship or to invite the crew to surrender and escape before bombs were placed in it. Another advantage of surfacing was that a clear distinction could be made between enemy ships and neutral ships, something that was impossible to discover looking through the periscope, especially when the ship had hoisted false colours.

The immediate reaction to the U-boat menace was to arm merchant ships with guns. This was not easy as guns were in such short supply, but Winston Churchill at the Admiralty improvised. 'The scarcity was such,' he said, 'that the guns had to be transferred from outward to inward bound vessels at ports outside the submarine zone so as to make them go further.' The next step was the use of Q-boats, which were introduced in 1915. These were merchant vessels, which were especially equipped with concealed guns firing from behind trap door bulwarks and fitted with torpedo tubes as well. Their function was to entice the U-boat towards them by pretending to panic and abandon ship, until the victim was within shooting distance. They had tolerable success, but were likely to be shot up before their chance came.

The decision, taken by the Germans in 1917, to wage unrestricted submarine warfare against all shipping, was a last desperate attempt to win the war. It had the effect of drawing the United States into the war, because it involved the indiscriminate sinking of all ships in British shipping lanes. This eventually gave the allies the crucial advantage in the war, but not before they had been given a fright. The German Naval Staff undertook to reduce British shipping at the rate of 600,000 tons a month, which they reckoned would cripple Great Britain within half a year. They did not achieve this target, but in the second quarter of 1917 they sank a monthly average of 400,000 tons of British shipping. In addition, they sank a similar tonnage of allied and neutral shipping as can be seen on the chart. By May 1917, the position was critical, but thereafter matters improved.

44 Shipping losses 1914–18. This diagram shows that the U-boat offensive against Allied shipping really became serious during the first half of 1917. Unrestricted U-boat warfare was declared by the Germans in January of that year but by the second quarter of 1918 the Allies were building more ships than they were losing.

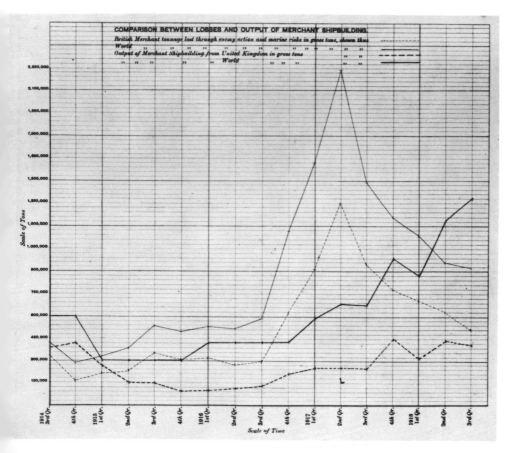

45 A convoy seen from an escort vessel. This system was adopted towards the end of the First World War and was used throughout the Second World War. The Admiralty provided a screen of destroyers armed with depth charges, which was a considerable deterrent to U-boats.

The reduction in shipping losses can be ascribed to the start of the convoy system in May 1917. It was not tried earlier because it was thought that a concentration of ships would merely present a larger target. In fact, it was later shown that the convoy greatly reduced the number of targets in a certain area and also made it easier for the Admiralty to provide a screen of destroyers armed with depth charges.

While English shipping was surviving this crisis, other countries were developing their trading fleets with far less danger and far more profit. The Americans had become so dependent on foreign ships to carry their trade before the war that the war made them embark upon a tremendous shipbuilding programme to supply their own ships. When the war was over, they had such a good fleet that they took measures to keep it. The Japanese also took advantage of the war to build up the shore organization for liner trades in the Far East and the Pacific Ocean, which had previously been dominated by British trading companies.

The small European countries like Norway, Denmark and Holland also survived the war somewhat better than Britain from the shipping point of view. They suffered severe losses from U-boat attacks and from their operations in the embattled areas of the North Sea, but they were able to profit from the high prices that the countries at war were prepared to pay for shipping. While British shipowners had to be content with the government's far from generous charter rates, these freelance traders could charge whatever they could get.

This had an effect when the time came to replace shipping losses. Ships were extremely expensive after the war as they were in very great demand, but British shipowners had no great profits on which to draw. Government compensation for shipping sunk was not generous either. The established lines spent, in making good their losses, twice the sum they received from the government under the special War Risk Insurance Scheme, in the estimate of one shipping historian. British shipowners had to make do with German ships that were taken over at the end of the war, and with purchases from foreign owners at inflated prices.

The shipping boom only continued while countries were restocking after the war. After two years of frantic trading, demand suddenly slackened. *The Economist* called 1921 'one of the worst years of depression since the industrial revolution'. From the point of view of shipping, it meant that 20 per cent of the world fleet was laid up. These slump conditions were not to disappear finally until after the Second World War.

The Slump

The worst period for British shipping was in the 1930s after the World Economic Crisis of 1931. There was a tremendous contraction in world trade which affected every nation, but none more than Great Britain which depended on trade for its livelihood. There was also a decline in international migration, which took away much of the work of the passenger liners, but it is in this field that British operators showed most enterprise and vision. It was in the 1930s that the keels of the two largest passenger ships were laid, the *Queen Mary* and the *Queen Elizabeth*. These were great luxury liners equipped with every device to make life comfortable. The *Queen Mary*, whose construction was delayed by the world economic situation in 1931, had 21 lifts, Turkish and curative baths, a shopping centre, banks and a garage among other amenities. Work was found for these liners by encouraging people to go on cruises to the West Indies and the Mediterranean as alternatives to seaside holidays.

The cargo liners and tramp steamers had no alternative to trade. They were to be seen laid up in the estuaries along the British coastline. The cargo liners suffered from the competition of the regular liner services, which were subsidized by foreign governments eager to encourage their own national merchant fleets. Competition between the liner companies became so intense that it was difficult for them to fill up their ships with specialised cargoes. They, therefore, were glad to fill their empty spaces with cheap, bulky cargoes, which would have normally been carried by tramp steamers.

Tramp shipping also suffered due to the continued decline in coal exports.

46 The *Queen Elizabeth*, launched in 1938 and taken out of service in 1968. She was used as a troop ship during the war, but from 1945 onwards, together with her sister ship the *Queen Mary*, sh worked as a passenger liner on the Atlantic.

This was the commodity which accounted for most of the volume of British trade, and there were no other bulky cargoes to replace it on the export side. Until 1914, British tramp shipping had held its own in the long-haul coal trades that involved voyages to countries outside Europe, and this had enabled it to dominate oceanic trade, for once in distant ports they were relied on to carry the bulky cargoes between ports in those areas. After the 1914–18 war, the volume of British exports declined steadily from 93.6 million tons in 1913 to only 49.7 million tons in 1938. Almost all the decline was in coal.

The new fuel that was in ever increasing demand was oil, but this was carried in special ships called tankers. Imports into this country of this commodity grew gradually so that, whereas in 1913 it accounted for one per cent of our total trade, in 1938 it accounted for ten per cent. Oil companies tended to have their own tanker fleets for their normal needs, but chartered private tankers to meet sudden increases in demand. One oil company, the Anglo-Saxon Oil Company, decided to depend entirely on chartered vessels and put its fleet of 37 tankers up for sale in 1926. Most of them were purchased by Norwegian owners, and from that time on Norway became the main home of tanker owners, who let them out on charter. British shipowners had only a small part in the charter side of oil tankers and were, therefore, left behind in the carriage of the new fuel.

Another factor in the decreasing competitiveness of the British tramp shipping was its slowness in installing Diesel engines. These internal combustion engines consumed less fuel for each horse power produced and thus were more economical. Our continental rivals realized this at a time when freight rates were so low that every penny counted. The typical British tramp was still a nine-knot coal-burning steamer even in 1939.

The result of the contraction of trade and the inability of British shipping to maintain its supremacy was the adoption by the British government of a policy of protection. In 1932, a tariff of ten per cent was placed on all manufactured foreign trade, and in 1935 tramp steamers were offered public assistance if voyages were undertaken at a freight charge lower than a certain standard rate. This marked the end of the era of Free Trade and the end of an era in British shipping. The period when British shipping and trade could hold their own in the world had really ended in 1914. The British shipping fleet had been slightly bigger then than it was in 1939.

The Second World War

The part played by the merchant marine in the Second World War was relatively more heroic than in the first World War. Whereas the casualties in the fighting services were much lower than in the 1914–18 war, the casualties in the Merchant Navy were more than double. Thirty-three thousand seamen lost their lives in this war. This was mainly due to the long period over which the U-boat offensive was mounted. Eight hundred thousand tons of shipping were lost in the first nine months of the war, before the German air attack on the ports had begun. It then continued at full strength until 1943, when it began to be brought under control. It was worst at the end of 1942, when ships were being sunk at a similar rate to the loss at the worst period in the First World War, and losses in March 1943 were the highest in either war. Matters improved thereafter, with the provision of American destroyers and the diversion of bombers to escort duty.

Although submarines were larger by the Second World War, they were still dependent on the atmosphere for driving their diesel engines, which meant that they could only be used when the submarine was surfaced. They had to depend on batteries when underwater and these never had enough storage capacity for prolonged operation. Towards the end of the Second World War, the Germans adopted an innovation in submarine design called the schnorkel, which was an air tube raised to the surface when the submarine was at periscope depth. This enabled the batteries to be recharged when the submarine was mainly hidden from view beneath the sea, but even then the submarine was still detectable by radar. It was only with the introduction of nuclear power, in the American submarine *Nautilus* in 1955, that submarines could operate underwater for indefinite periods. The nuclear reactor produces heat to turn water into steam, which in turn drives the main propulsion turbines. No air is needed for this process so that nuclear submarines can now cruise round the world permanently submerged.

Great Britain experienced an acute shortage of shipping from the very beginning of the Second World War. The necessity of grouping ships into convoys caused delays which reduced their carrying capacity by 20 to 25 per cent. The transportation of wheeled vehicles and tanks to the Middle East took away a large number of ships from normal trades. Winston Churchill said, 'It is the vehicles that take the shipping space out of all proportion to the other needs of the fighting men.' Space was saved by sending them over in pieces for assembly at their destination, but this was never very popular with the troops. Another problem was caused by the closure of the ports on the east coast in 1940 to all but the smallest boats, due to the danger from enemy air attack. The western ports took some time to adapt to the new volume of trade and even they came under air attack in 1941.

The size of the merchant fleet was increased by chartering the fleets of the countries overrun by Hitler, such as Norway, Denmark and Holland. Their reluctance to hand themselves over was overcome by a ship warrant scheme, by which only warranted ships could use the ports of the British Commonwealth. In fact, mutually acceptable terms were worked out on the principle of equality of reward and sacrifice with the Norwegian and Dutch fleets. Once again the home mercantile marine was chartered by the government, but this time the foreign rivals were not in a position to take advantage of high freight rates as they were mostly involved in the war. Of the American fleet, it was said that it constantly increases while the British diminishes, but the Americans were our allies and loaned us any shipping that was surplus to their requirements.

The worst period for British and British-controlled shipping was in 1942, when Hitler was at the height of his success and the Americans had become involved in the war with Japan in the Pacific. In the winter of 1942–43, imports had to be confined to absolute essentials; cuts were made in foodstuffs so that animal feed, fruit and vegetables were virtually eliminated and sugar imports were cut by half. Winston Churchill warned the American President in March 1943, 'Unless we can get a satisfactory long-term settlement, British ships will have to be withdrawn from their present military service, even though our agreed operations are crippled or prejudiced.'

At the peace, however, the British shipping industry was in a much more favourable position than it had been in 1918. All but 3.6 million tons of the 11 million tons lost during the war had been replaced by wartime building, by purchases from the U.S.A., or by ships allocated to the United Kingdom by the Inter Allied Reparations Agency. The American ships acquired were Liberty ships, which had been mass-produced in large numbers. Over 2,600 were built in a manner never seen before, with huge sub-assemblies constructed off the ways,

47 A Liberty ship being unloaded in North Africa, in the Second World War. Produced by the Americans by assembly line methods, there are no rivets to be seen in the hull as the sub-assemblies were welded together. This picture also shows the sansom posts, which rise like a letter T from the deck. From the sansom post derricks are swung, which act as cranes for loading and unloading.

and with welding used almost exclusively. They were oil-fired steamers of 7,000 tons, which served well as tramp shipping. The 1939 tonnage was not passed until 1954, but at least Britain's merchant fleet was in better shape than that of most of its rivals.

War and slump had therefore created great difficulty for British shipping between 1914 and 1945. Great Britain was still the largest shipping nation after the Second World War was over, but it had been giving ground to its rivals year by year. In 1945, however, all the Great Powers were suffering from the same war weariness and weakness, so that there was a long period of retrenchment before post-war trade began to revive.

British losses and gains 1942 and 1943
(Dry-cargo ship 1,600 gross tons and over)

Date	British-controlled Ships (Thousand tons gross)		
	Gains	Losses	Net gain or loss
1942			
January-February	546	757	—211
April-June	607	892	—285
July-September	822	980	—158
October-December	626	1,334	—708
1943			
January-March	542	722	—180
April-June	643	437	+206
July-September	830	389	+441
October-December	338	266	+ 72

7 Ships and Cargoes

Definitions

Comparison in the size of ships according to their weight has always been hazardous due to the different meanings of the word 'tonnage'. It has never been an expression of the weight of a cargo ship, but has always expressed its carrying capacity. Displacement tonnage, which reflects the pure weight of a ship, is only relevant to naval combatant vessels. Originally tonnage meant the capacity of a vessel to hold tuns of wine, a tun measuring 42 cubic feet. Nowadays it has three possible meanings as far as cargo ships are concerned. Gross tonnage is a space measurement, one gross ton being equal to 100 cubic feet of permanently enclosed space and is the system used to describe passenger and cargo ships. This is the tonnage usually used in this book.

Net tonnage is a measure of carrying capacity. It is the gross tonnage minus the cubic capacity of non-earning spaces like crew space, engine rooms, fuel and ballast. This tonnage is usually used in calculating port and canal dues.

Deadweight tonnage is generally used in describing tankers and other bulk carriers, and is the actual weight in tons of cargo and fuel that a ship can carry when down to her load line. There is no direct relation between deadweight and gross tonnage, but a rough rule of thumb is that 1,000 gross tons are equivalent to 1,600 deadweight tons. The *Queen Elizabeth* at 83,673 tons would therefore be equivalent in size to a tanker of about 135,000 deadweight tons.

The load-line is the Plimsoll line on the side of the ship, put there by the Board of Trade to ensure that ships always have a certain amount of reserve buoyancy when fully loaded. The Plimsoll mark is a circle with a line through it, which represents the safety line in summer. Forward of this mark are a series of alternative lines, taking into account the differing densities of water when it is cold or fresh. There may be a further series of lines nearer the stern, which are the timber load lines. This cargo is so buoyant that timber ships are permitted to load deeper.

Lloyd's Register of Shipping is another guarantee of the maintenance of standards in shipping. From its foundation in 1760, the Register was a useful adjunct to the insurance of shipping. It is printed annually and contains the names, classes and other useful information relating to ships classed by Lloyds; it also includes as far as possible the names and particulars of all other sea-going merchant ships of the world of 100 tons and over. Ships which pass the tests are classed as 100A1, which is a guarantee of quality until the next periodic survey, which is required at four-yearly intervals.

48 The *Queen Elizabeth 2*, the new Cunarder launched in 1967. This photograph of her was taken during her trials off the island of Arran, Scotland. The ship's service speed is $28\frac{1}{2}$ knots and she has a passenger capacity of 2,025 people. Her draught of $32\frac{1}{2}$ feet will enable her to pass through the Suez and Panama Canals.

Passenger Liners

These are the big ships on which the prestige of the big shipping companies is based. They also become objects of national pride as names such as *France* and *United States* indicate. The state normally subsidizes this kind of ship, as they do not readily attract investment and they are very useful as troop carriers in time of war. The *Queen Elizabeth* and the *Queen Mary* did very useful work in troop transport in the Second World War and the *United States* was built to specifications approved by the American Army so that it could fulfil this function in case of need.

Passenger liners are no longer as vast as they were between the wars. The *Queen Mary* remains the largest liner ever built. The reason for their more moderate size since then is that there has been no indication that passenger traffic by sea will increase very much. The number of passengers crossing the Atlantic fell from 2.6 million in 1913 (all by sea), to 0.66 million in 1937 (almost all by sea). In 1958, the total was 2.25 million (just under one million by sea and just over one million by air). The great new competitor is the aircraft, which transported over half of the total Atlantic passenger traffic in 1957 and will take a still greater proportion now that the Jumbo Jets are in service. The construction of the *Queen Elizabeth 2* by the Cunard Steam Ship Company in 1967 was an act of faith which many thought foolhardy, after the two former Queens had been sold to America as permanently anchored pleasure grounds.

49 The *Northern Star*. This passenger liner and her sister ship the *Southern Cross* are unusual in that they have their engines and funnel at the stern. The *Northern Star* was completed in 1962, and has a gross tonnage of 24,756 tons and a speed of 20 knots.

There are many passenger liners of around 20,000 tons, which can be termed big ships. These are well fitted to the passenger demand on the regular routes, and normally they carry cargo as well. The Union Castle Line, which dominates the South Africa route, has one of the largest fleets of big ships with six ships of over 20,000 tons. The *Windsor Castle*, which began service in 1960, is the largest at 37,640 tons, with accommodation for 882 passengers.

The development of cruising as an alternative to the passenger trade began in the 1930s and has grown since the war. The Shaw Savill Line has elaborated this idea by providing four round-the-world voyages every year. It has two large liners which carry only passengers; they are the *Southern Cross* and the *Northern Star*. These ships are unusual also in that they have their engines and funnel at the stern of the ship, as in a tanker. This has certain advantages in the lay-out of the deck, which is not divided into two by the funnel. It makes it possible to provide large play areas and a fine promenade. Another variation on the cruise is the educational voyage in the Mediterranean and Baltic Seas, which has been started by the British India Steam Navigation Company. Short visits to places of interest on land are interspersed with lectures on board connected with those places, which makes it a true extension of classroom teaching.

Cargo Ships

A distinction was made between cargo liners and tramp steamers up to the end of the Second World War, but since then the categories have become somewhat different. There are now three main classes of cargo boat: the general cargo ship, equipped to deal with a varied cargo for a number of destinations; the bulk carrier to take loose commodities such as fertiliser and grain, which has superseded the tramp steamer; and the tanker which mainly carries oil. These categories are by no means hard and fast. Indeed, there is a clear move by shipowners to build ships which can fulfil any of a number of functions. There are multi-purpose bulk carriers called o.b.o. ships (short for Oil, Bulk grain or fertilizer and Ore). These ships with flexible functions will enable the shipowner to use his ship in whichever trade is flourishing at the time. Eventualities like the closing of the Suez Canal or the destruction of a pipe line create a sudden demand for tankers, which can be a source of great profit if the shipowner has the right ships available.

General cargo ships are never very big as they are part of a regular service, the attraction of which is that it is frequent and dependable. They are usually no bigger than 10,000 tons. They have a distinctive superstructure of sansom posts and derricks, which are there to help with loading and unloading. The derrick is a pole surmounted by a pulley block, which is capable of lifting around ten tons. It swings from the sansom post, which looks like a short, stout mast and is able to lift goods from the hold and deposit them on the quay. At least one of the derricks must be capable of lifting the much heavier articles that are sometimes carried, because not all ports have floating cranes capable of lifting weights over 20 tons.

The hold is the cargo space within the ship, and the hole which gives access to it from the deck is called the hatch. The hatch used to be covered in with boards, which in turn were covered by tarpaulin, but nowadays they are fitted with modern hatch covers, which lift in one piece or fold up like a concertina.

The holds in a cargo liner are separate and devoted to varying functions. Temperature and humidity can be controlled with great accuracy so that cargoes of all kinds can be carried with safety. Refrigeration is one of the most important techniques. In the first refrigerated ships the cargo was packed in ice, which made it very unpleasant to handle, but now a cold-air system is used in which the refrigeration machinery reduces the temperature of brine circulating in pipes. Brine is salt water, which has a lower freezing temperature than ordinary water and is very easily prepared. The temperature of the air can be controlled very accurately, so that apples and oranges can be kept at a temperature that varies by no more than two degrees, and beef can be chilled at a temperature of 28° F. Bulk carriers need no derricks or cranes as in most cases the cargo can be discharged by suction machinery, or in the case of coal or mineral ore, by grabs. There are, however, bulk cargoes, which present problems of their own. Some, like tallow, vegetable oil, molasses and asphalt, need to be kept hot by a series of

50 This is the *British Explorer*, the first of seven 215,000 deadweight ton, crude-oil tankers being built in Japan for British Petroleum. She is moving into her fitting-out berth at Nagasaki.

pipes through which steam is passed so that they do not solidify. But in the case of methane from the Sahara desert, the temperature must be kept at —258° F. so that the gas remains in a liquid state. In this state it takes up only one six-hundredth of the space that the same weight of gas would occupy.

Live animals, and cars, present particular problems of their own. Animals need special ships which can cater for their feeding needs and the cleaning of their stalls on the journey. Cars often go as general cargo, but they are very space consuming. Some bulk carriers are fitted with a series of collapsible floors which hinge down from the roof so that the whole hold can be filled with cars. Alternatively, with the floors out of the way, they can take on a normal bulk product.

Tankers are distinctive ships which are little more than an oil-tight tank of oil propelled by an engine on the back. The first tanker was the *Gluckauf*, which was built at Newcastle-on-Tyne for a German owner in 1886, and since then they have become more and more numerous. There is no practical limitation on their size except their ability to make the journey and to discharge their cargo. The larger the tanker, the greater the depth of water needed to keep it buoyant, so the depth of the Suez Canal and of the home port have always been limiting factors. The principle that 'the greater the size, the cheaper the product at its

51 The container ship *Jervis Bay* loading at the No. 39 container dock at Tilbury. The letters O.C.L. stand for Overseas Containers Limited and the letters A.C.T. for Associated Container Transportation. This berth provides a container service to Australia.

52 The *Acadia Forest*, the world's first LASH (Lighter Aboard Ship) in the Medway in 1969. Looking like an enormous barge she carries 73 rectangular lighters, loaded with containers. Tugs take these to the ship and manoeuvre them into the stern loading bay. Then they are loaded on deck or lowered into the holds by the ship's travelling crane.

destination' has driven shipowners to build larger and larger tankers, and now monsters of 190,000 deadweight tons are being built in Japan. Ever since the Suez Canal was closed by the Arab-Israeli War in 1967, tankers have been bound to take the longer route, and on that route it is no disadvantage to be huge. Oil companies are quite prepared to transfer the oil from the giant tankers to smaller ones in the Channel, so that there is no need for them to come close inshore. The loading and unloading of tankers is now so rapid that their crews complain that there is no time for shore leave during the turn round.

Container Ships

The next stage in shipping has already begun with the container revolution. Much of the expense of carrying freight occurs at the docks, when time lost means extra port dues and all the cost of paying the dockers another day's wages to unload. This precious time can be saved if the cargo is packed into large boxes called containers. The first step towards this practice was the scheme for 'unitised' cargoes, by which sacks or lengths of timber were tied into bundles of a size that could be easily handled by a derrick or crane. Containers, however, are a far

73

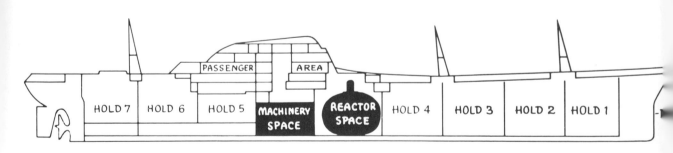

PASSENGER AREA

HOLD 7 · HOLD 6 · HOLD 5 · MACHINERY SPACE · REACTOR SPACE · HOLD 4 · HOLD 3 · HOLD 2 · HOLD 1

53 The *Savannah*, an experimental nuclear merchant ship built in America, which first crossed the Atlantic in 1964. Before this journey, the ship travelled 25,000 miles on two pounds of uranium. To cover a similar distance a conventional ship of similar size would have used 6,500 tons of oil fuel. It is designed to carry 60 passengers and 746,000 cubic feet of cargo at a speed of 20 knots. The plan of the ship (below) shows how little space is taken up by the engine and reactor.

more radical move as they need to be handled by specially designed ships. The quay must also have a gantry that can lift the container from the chassis of a container lorry on the quayside onto the deck of the ship. As all the containers are the same height and width, the organisation of the stowing of the hold becomes a straightforward routine as does the unloading. The container ship can therefore hope to be away from the quay within 24 hours.

An even more revolutionary ship is the *Acadia Forest,* which is owned by Mosvold Shipping of Norway and is the world's first L.A.S.H. (Lighter Aboard Ship). It is 850 feet long and has the appearance of a gigantic canal barge. The ship carries 73 rectangular barges loaded with containers. These are towed to the vessel by tugs, which nudge them into her stern lifting bay, where they are handled by the ship's travelling crane, which lifts them to their position on board. Lighters can be loaded at a rate of one every 15 minutes, making a total of 18 hours for the whole operation, which ensures a quick turn-round. It could be a very useful ship for London, where much of the cargo is handled by barges already.

The Future

A ship of the future is the nuclear ship. The United Kingdom has postponed construction until a reactor can be developed that offers some hope of economy in operation comparable to that of a merchant ship powered by oil. The first nuclear ship was the Russian icebreaker *Lenin,* which was built in 1959 to keep the route to the Russian Arctic ports open for a little longer in the summer. The first nuclear merchant ship was the *Savannah,* namesake of the first steamer to cross the Atlantic, and which first crossed the Atlantic itself in 1964. It was very much an experimental ship, for the training of technicians in the techniques of handling nuclear ships, as well as a cargo boat. Its great advantage is its economy on fuel. It sailed for 330,000 miles during $3\frac{1}{2}$ years before it needed its new fuel of enriched uranium oxide.

Another invention which has implications for the future is the introduction of automatic control systems. These enable the captain of the ship to control all the functions of the ship from the navigating bridge, so that he is no longer dependent upon giving instructions to the engine room from the bridge. The Japanese are furthest advanced in this kind of automation, and first introduced it in 1961. There are similar moves towards automatic steering so that a ship without a crew may be possible in the future, though it is probable that there will always be a need for skilled technicians. As in almost every other branch of industrial activity, the jobs involving plain hard work are being taken over by machines.

8 Docks and Ports

London Docks

In a parliamentary debate in 1656, it was said of a bill benefiting the city that 'it seems that this London must have all the trade'. This certainly seemed to be the case in the 17th century, and even at the end of the 18th century it handled about 65 per cent by value of the country's total imports and exports. It has already been noticed that the Western ports, such as Bristol and Liverpool, were beginning to develop trade of their own by that time, but it is only since the 18th century that they have accounted for a substantial proportion of British trade. At the present time, London handles 32 per cent of British trade by value and Liverpool 21 per cent, so that London is no longer nearly so dominant.

At the end of the 18th century, London still had no docks, unless private ventures like Howland Dock of 1700 or the Brunswick Dock of 1789 are counted. The ships were unloaded at timber wharves, that jutted out into the river, and the goods were handled at the river side or in the warehouses that lined the banks. This arrangement had certain disadvantages. The first was that the City of London enjoyed a monopoly of the wharves and tended to limit their number for the sake of larger profit. All foreign goods had to be handled at these 'legal quays' and such was the shortage of berths at times that there was serious congestion and delay. Another difficulty was the prevalence of stealing on the river. The ships, the barges into which goods were off-loaded, and the quayside were open to the river, thus enabling thieves to make an easy living by rowing to the quayside and awaiting their chance to thieve from the cargo. There was a cunning trade called mudlarking, by which dockers were bribed to drop goods overboard as they unloaded, often with ropes and markers attached so that they could readily be retrieved. The mudlarkers would then grapple for the goods or search for them in the mud at low tide.

These shortcomings of the old system led merchants to seek authority by Act of Parliament to build enclosed docks. Only in this way could they provide adequate protection for their cargoes and avoid the delays on the 'legal quays'. The first major dock was the West India Dock, completed in 1802. It was divided from the river by single gates, which were opened only at high tide when the river level rose to the same height as that of the dock. This meant that ships in dock could lie safely while unloading, but could only leave or enter at high tide.

Other docks followed in quick succession. The London Docks were opened in 1805, the East India Docks in 1806, the St. Katharine Docks in 1828; the Surrey Commercial Docks, though started in 1807, were added to throughout the 19th century. The expansion of the docks continued at a more leisurely rate throughout the century with the opening of the Victoria Dock in 1855, the Millwall Docks in 1868, and the Royal Albert Dock in 1880. Further down the river the Tilbury Docks were opened in 1886. These docks were all fitted with double canal gates so that ships could enter and depart, whatever the state of the tide.

A convention that was quickly accepted in the docks was the right of barges to enter and leave the docks without the payment of dues. This became known as the 'Free Water Clause', because it was incorporated into all the Acts of Parliament authorizing the construction of further docks on the Thames. It helps to explain why London has become a barge port. About 75 per cent of the port's trade is handled by inland water transport carrying cargo to wharves along the Thames. Barges are to be seen at all parts of the tidal portion of the Thames, lying at their moorings or being pulled along in groups by a tug.

During the 19th century, ownership of the docks was shared among a number of companies who competed for business both among themselves and with the wharf-owners along the Thames. Competition was so fierce that some dock

54 The Royal Docks, London. The Royal Victoria (foreground), the Royal Albert (far left) and the King George V (far right) together have a water area of 230 acres. They form the largest man-made sheet of dock water in the world. They have a total length of eleven miles of quay, which provide 52 deep water berths.

55 The familiar sight of barges on the Thames. Barges can enter and leave the docks freely, so that London has become a barge port. The barges carry port-cargoes to wharves along the Thames and bring cargoes to the ship's side. There are some 4,800 in daily use in the port. Most of them are without means of powered propulsion so they are towed to their destination by tugs.

companies, having lowered their charges to keep in line with the others, found that they were running at a loss. There were some aspects of river management over which the whole port had to collaborate. The most important was the need to keep the channels along the river dredged and deepened as the size of ships entering the port increased. It was these considerations that persuaded opinion that a single authority for the whole port was needed. The Port of London Authority was established by the Port of London Act of 1908. It was to be responsible for the control of the tidal waters of the River Thames from the estuary to Teddington, and it was to take over the powers of the existing dock companies. Its control was not complete as the riverside wharves remained outside its authority, but it did manage all the enclosed dock accommodation and the deep water channel into the port.

Each group of docks has its own character. The St. Katharine Docks, which are now closed, and the London Docks are associated with warehousing. Barges bring cargoes, which have been discharged down river at the larger docks, for storage here, though these docks handle smaller ships themselves. The main commodities stored are wool, which will eventually be laid out for public auction, and wine, which is laid in the vaults. The Millwall and India Docks have been extensively modernized in recent years. The Millwall Docks have transit sheds with large working areas where fork-lift trucks can be used with advantage, and a berth which caters for side loading. A transit shed is a one-storey covered area where goods can be laid while they are being transferred from the ship to road or rail transport or vice versa, and side-loading is a far more convenient method of filling or emptying the ship's hold through a hatch in the side, rather than through a hatch on the deck.

The Surrey Docks specialize in timber and maintain the connection which England has always had with the Baltic. The largest docks, however, are in the Royal group further downstream. They form, in fact, the largest enclosed dock in the world, providing 11 miles of quay and 52 deep water berths. Their most recent addition was the King George V Dock built in 1921. The southern side of this dock is made up of seven dolphins or jetties. This arrangement allows barges to moor between the dolphin and the quay, so that the cranes mounted on the dolphins can discharge cargo either into the barges or onto the quay with equal ease. The other docks also employ modern new equipment which reduces cargo-handling to the minimum. The Royal Victoria has elaborate resources for handling grain. Fixed elevators can transfer the grain straight from the ship to the granaries by suction, or floating elevators can deliver it over the side into barges. It also has facilities for unloading meat and transferring the carcasses onto rail or barge transport automatically. The Royal Albert has a fully-mechan-ised banana berth, which can transfer the fruit gently by conveyor belt from the ship's hold to land transport. In addition, the Royal Docks handle an important proportion of the country's manufactured goods for export.

56 The Port of London; the installations under its control are shaded on the lower map. The Tilbury Docks are much nearer to the sea than the older docks and they are the present growth area. On the upper map the water areas of the dock area are marked as docks. The rest of the shaded area is merely the land under the control of the P.L.A.

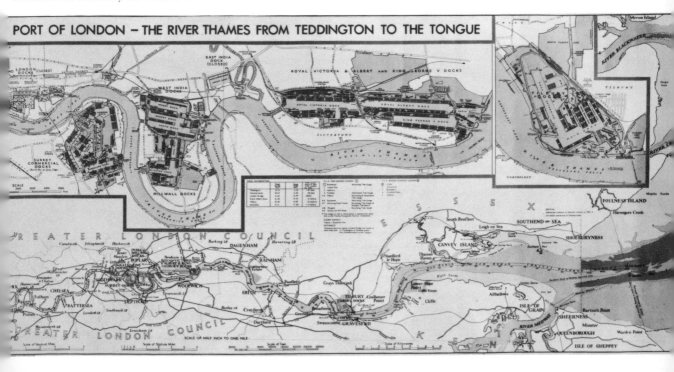

PORT OF LONDON – THE RIVER THAMES FROM TEDDINGTON TO THE TONGUE

57 A floating crane. The Port of London has a fleet of heavy floating cranes for lifting cargoes beyond the capacity of normal quay cranes. These cranes can lift weights of up to 200 tons. This picture shows the *London Leviathan*.

Arrival and Departure

Ships have to follow a set routine as they approach the Port of London. Out at sea, a sea pilot boards the ship to guide it either by the North or South Channel into the estuary. At Gravesend, he hands over the ship to a river pilot who is responsible for directing the ship to the dock gate. Here also, the ship will be boarded by the Customs and Excise men and tugs will be engaged to draw the ship upstream, if it is large. Already the shipping company will have arranged a berth with the Authority, so that the Dockmaster will be ready to receive the ship at the dock entrance. The lock serves both as an entrance and an exit. The ship will therefore have to wait until the lock is free and then enter only on the Dockmaster's instructions.

The berth to which the ship is directed will be matched to the needs of the cargo, and the shipowner will also have made clear whether he wants the cargo transhipped into barges or landed on the quays. The Authority will also want to know whether the quayside goods are for immediate delivery, that is, for direct transfer onto land transport, or whether they are to go into a warehouse for storage.

Once the ship is unloaded, it is likely to move directly onto a new berth for reloading. The start of a loading programme must also be arranged between the Authority and the shipowner. The cargo will begin to be accumulated in a transit shed three or four days before loading begins. The shipowner will have to inform his likely customers by post or by advertisement that the ship is about to sail and invite them to send their goods to the appropriate shed. As a cargo liner will normally make several calls on its route, the order of loading is most important. An added complication is that some cargo arrives by barge and is loaded straight onto the ship. It therefore demands great concentration and co-ordination to ensure that the goods to be off-loaded at the first port of call are loaded last. The closing date for receiving cargo is normally two or three days before the ship sails, to enable the loading programme to be completed without mishap.

Quay cranes and ship derricks are normally of from three to five tons capacity and can handle most kinds of general cargo. When there is a really heavy article, like a locomotive, one of the Authority's heavy floating cranes is used. The Authority has six of them, the largest being the *London Mammoth* which can lift weights of 200 tons to a height of 135 feet. There are ship's derricks in existence which are capable of lifting similar loads, so the ship can sometimes depend on its own resources.

58 'Dolphins'. This is the name given to a jetty which is divided from the quay by a channel wide enough for barges. This arrangement was incorporated into the design of the south side of the King George V Dock at London in 1921. It enables barges to be loaded from the quay without interfering with the shipwork of the cranes mounted on the dolphins. The cranes can easily span the barge road.

59 The Manchester Ship Canal. This canal is the only entrance to the port of Manchester and is wide enough for two ships to pass. Notice that the ships are propelled by tugs.

Other British Ports

London is essentially a cargo port, but it does have facilities for receiving passenger ships at Tilbury opposite Gravesend. Passengers disembark with their luggage at the Tilbury Landing Stage, which can accommodate ships whatever the state of the tide. The ship can then proceed to the appropriate dock to discharge its cargo. The most important passenger terminal, however, is Southampton, which is a terminal for the world's largest liners. The port has the advantage of a complicated tidal flow, which gives the estuary four tides instead of two and reduces the maximum rise and fall of the water to around 13 feet. There is no need, therefore, for the usual locks and the docks are open to the sea. The most celebrated quay is the Ocean Terminal, which is used by the *Queens*. Another important passenger port is Liverpool, where the Princes Landing Stage provides a quay one-third of a mile long, capable of handling the longest liners.

Liverpool, at the mouth of the River Mersey, is Britain's second port. The docks are controlled by the Mersey Docks and Harbour Board, which is also responsible for the smaller ports like Birkenhead on the other side of the river. The docks are enclosed as in London, but one big difference is the relative absence of barge traffic. The port is too near to the open sea for such cumbersome river craft to be handled with complete safety. Another difference is that the usual berth is on a jetty rather than on a straight quay.

The River Mersey gives access to another very large port at Manchester. This is approached by way of the Manchester Ship Canal, which starts from the south bank of the river not far from Liverpool. The canal is 36 miles long and provides a channel for ocean-going ships to inland docks on the outskirts of the city. The original project was bitterly opposed by Liverpool, but was loyally supported by subscriptions from the Manchester area. It took some time to pay its way, but it has enabled Manchester to become one of the principal British ports, although it is well inland.

Of the other Western ports, only Glasgow and Bristol are of any size. Like Southampton, Glasgow has the advantage of being a port open to the sea as the estuary of the River Clyde provides natural deep water anchorages. Bristol has suffered a relative decline since the 18th century because it has not become an industrial centre of such magnitude as the Lancashire towns or Glasgow.

There are strong indications that the relative importance of the British ports may change in the near future, mainly due to the strong organization of the dockers in the ports of London and Liverpool which enables them to demand high wages by the threat of strikes. The dockers' unions also frantically resist schemes which increase efficiency by mechanization for fear of the subsequent loss of jobs. There is a strong temptation, therefore, for shipping companies introducing new labour-saving methods, like containerization, to centre them on a new port rather than on an old one. Southampton is being chosen by container companies for exactly this reason, and is likely to become an important cargo port as well as the leading passenger port. The Cunard Company has moved their headquarters to Southampton, Atlantic Container Lines have started their new container and wheeled cargo service there and the container service to the Far East, which is to start in 1971, will be operated from there.

The next logical move in the management of British ports is to bring them under state control and a single directing authority. A Bill was under consideration in Parliament in late 1969, which would have established a National Ports Authority to control all ports which handle over five million tons of shipping a year. The Authority would have been responsible for almost all British trade and would have worked through a series of subsidiary authorities, established to replace the present port authorities. It was hoped that dock labour would share more in the administration of the ports through their own local dock labour committees. British docks certainly need to develop a better relationship between management and workers.

The Bill involved the nationalisation of all major ports and was opposed by the Conservative Party, which dislikes any measure that limits competition. The Bill was withdrawn when the Conservatives won the 1970 election and the whole issue of port nationalisation will therefore probably be shelved for some time to come.

83

9 The Prosperous Age

Post-war Trade

The aftermath of the Second World War was very different from that of the First. The post-war boom was less pronounced and better sustained. When it seemed to be receding in 1949–50, it was quickly revived by the demands of the Korean War, which lasted until 1953. The recession that followed was not too deep, and movement out of it was helped by an artificial scarcity caused by the blocking of the Suez Canal in 1956 as a result of the Arab-Israeli War and the intervention by British and French paratroopers. The enforced use of the longer route round the Cape meant that more ships had to be employed to carry the same amount of trade. The Arab-Israeli War of 1967 had the same result, for this time the eastern bank was occupied permanently by the Israelis, which has meant that the Canal has not been used since. This has created a great demand for shipping and has provided a great incentive to build larger ships, so that the

60 A view of The Suez Canal, about halfway along. Since its opening in 1869 it has provided a short route from the Atlantic Ocean to the Indian Ocean. But as a result of the war between Israel and Egypt in 1967, the Canal was closed to oil companies who had used it as a route to the oil fields in the Persian Gulf. The monument on the right is the memorial to the dead of the Second World War.

extra costs of the longer route can be better offset. At the same time, it has been a period of steady growth in world trade; world trade doubled between 1948 and 1958, and has expanded at a similar rate ever since.

The profitability of trade enabled shipowners to replace their war losses and obsolete tonnage without having to borrow new capital. Until 1957, the market was so certain that shipowners could arrange a charter with an oil company, have the ship built to meet the exact specifications of the route and then sit back to enjoy the profits once the ship was built. In 1957, this dream evaporated when there was a recession, which began to leave much shipping without work. By mid-1959, the depression was such that nine per cent of the world fleet was idle, but even so it was nothing compared with the situation in the 1930s.

Although the British mercantile fleet has continued to grow gradually year by year, it has only grown slowly in relation to the world fleet as a whole. Between 1958 and 1968, the size of the British mercantile fleet increased from 20.2 million gross tons to 21.9 million tons, but during the same period, Britain's share of the world fleet dropped from 17 to 11 per cent. In 1968, an indication of further changes to come was reflected in the fact that the British fleet was no longer the biggest in the world. The first position was taken by Liberia, which is not a true shipping nation, but in 1969, Japan, as a genuine shipping nation, edged ahead of Britain and, if Japanese growth is maintained, Japan's mercantile marine may soon overtake Liberia's in size. The United States' merchant fleet is in fifth place, but this is not a true position as it has a reserve fleet of 8 million tons ready in case of war, but not in active use. Lloyds Register of Shipping gave the following totals for the gross tonnage of the top seven shipping nations in 1969:

Liberia	29,215,151
Japan	23,987,079
United Kingdom	23,843,799
Norway	19,679,094
U.S.A.	19,550,394
U.S.S.R.	13,704,604
Greece	8,580,753

Two features of British trade in the 1930s were still prevalent after the war. The first of these was a reluctance to keep pace with the growing demand for oil tankers. British oil imports increased almost four times between 1939 and 1960, while the British tanker fleet did little more than double its size. British tankers also tended to be smaller than the world average, because British shipowners were conscious of the limitations of the British oil terminals in handling the largest tankers. The second feature is the decreasing volume of British exports. As the export of coal declined even more, there was no weighty bulk product to take its place in the export trade. The volume of imports continued to grow however, as oil imports increased and had come to account for one half of the weight of all British imports. The position now, therefore, is that the goods imported into this country are four times as heavy as the exports.

61 An oil tanker afloat. This is the *Esso London,* flagship of Esso Petroleum, which was launched in 1963. She has an overall length of 855 feet and a deadweight tonnage of 90,173 tons. She is driven by a steam turbine which gives her a service speed of 17 knots.

62 The B.P. Tanker Company's ship *British Vigilance* is caught in the frozen ice of the Baltic, north of Sweden. Ships have to face such hazards all the time; in this case an ice-breaker had to clear a path into the port.

Flags of Convenience and Flag Discrimination

The term 'Flags of Convenience' is commonly used to describe the flags of such countries as Panama, Liberia and Honduras, whose laws allow ships owned by foreign shipowners to fly these flags. Although Liberia has now the largest merchant fleet in the world, virtually none of her ships are owned by Liberian subjects. The vast majority belong to American and Greek owners, who do not want to sail under their own flags.

The reasons for registering in Liberia are partly to avoid taxation, but here it must be remembered that whereas Liberian taxation is light, shipowners also forfeit any tax relief or benefits offered by their home government. In the case of American owners, they wish to avoid high American wage costs and laws that insist that 75 per cent of the crews and 100 per cent of the officers of American ships must be American nationals. If they are to employ cheaper foreign labour, American operators have to sail under a foreign flag. There are other advantages to be gained, as most developed countries have laws regarding manning scales, wage rates and social service payments, which put up the cost of labour in comparison with underdeveloped countries which have no such welfare legislation. It is not possible for Panholib (a diminutive of Panama, Honduras and Liberia) ships to cut too many corners in this respect, as they must always pass as safe for insurance purposes and meet the requirements of all the ports that they visit.

Most British ships sail under the British flag, although there was a move to use the Bermudan flag by a few. The reason for British loyalty to the flag is partly traditional, but more recently the government has given the shipping industry more incentive to remain British. There can be no doubt that enlightened taxation policy, especially in the form of encouragement to replace old ships and to finance new ones, has made it worth remaining British.

From the government's point of view, the shipping industry is one of the nation's most valuable assets. If flags are ignored and ships are attributed according to their ownership, the British merchant fleet is easily the largest in the world. It is also a most important invisible export earner. Invisible exports are those services, such as insurance or the carriage of goods for another country, which earn money for the country but are assessed separately from the visible exports, which are the actual goods which are exported. In 1968, the shipping industry made a substantial contribution of £262 million to the balance of payments, which is the balance between what we earn from exports and spend on imports.

As the United Kingdom still acts as a universal carrier of any country's trade, it is important to its health that the nations of the world should not reserve their own trade for their own ships. Such reservation of trade for the ships of one nation is called flag discrimination, and it is a practice that the Americans have followed since the First World War. The Americans also maintain liner services on all essential routes to and from the United States and the operators receive grants from the public funds designed to equate their costs with the rest of the world. Similar policies are followed by most South American countries, by India and Pakistan and by the Communist countries, but it does not necessarily involve all their trade. It is probable that about five per cent of world trade is not open to free competition.

British Trade Policy

There was, in fact, a concerted effort after the war by most of the world to keep tariffs as low as possible, so that the worst evils of protectionism between the wars could be avoided. Many countries signed the General Agreement on Tariffs and Trade (G.A.T.T.) in 1947 with the object of lowering duties product by product. This process was hastened when the G.A.T.T. members started negotiations called the Kennedy Round in 1964. They were named after President Kennedy, who envisaged it as part of a Grand Design for an Atlantic partnership. Their object was to effect a general reduction of tariffs of 50 per cent at least. Agreement was reached in 1967, but although there were agreed cuts of up to 50 per cent on industrial products, the reductions averaged just over 30 per cent on trade between the participating countries. The reductions were to be phased over five years so that they would not be fully effective until 1972. These cuts are very much in the interests of Great Britain as a shipping nation and Britain now shows more enthusiasm for them than the Americans.

Another factor affecting British trade is the development of the European Economic Community (E.E.C.) since 1957. It consists of Belgium, the Netherlands, Luxembourg, France, Italy and West Germany and is also known as the Common Market or The Six. Its object is to form a free trade area, which will be surrounded by a tariff wall to the outside world. The E.E.C. has signed the Kennedy Round Agreement, so the tariff wall will not be high, but it will make British goods a little less competitive in the six countries. This is serious, as the E.E.C. is Britain's closest market and Britain's trade with it has been growing faster than trade with other traditional trading areas like the Commonwealth. Britain joined an alternative trading association when it declined membership of the Common Market (E.E.C.) in 1957, and this is called the European Free Trade Area (E.F.T.A.). which consists of Denmark, Norway, Sweden, Switzerland, Austria and Portugal, in addition to Great Britain. It merely aims to lower tariffs for each of the members, without establishing a common tariff policy nor has it any of the implications of eventual political union which is implicit in the E.E.C.

A very powerful debate is developing over whether or not Britain should join the Common Market. All the main political parties are in support of Britain's entry, but each of them has minorities which oppose the idea. Opinion Polls reveal that public opinion ebbs first one way and then the other. The economic arguments seem to be slightly in favour of entry, as the Common Market's rate of economic growth seems to be faster than that of E.F.T.A. or the Commonwealth.

Moreover, there is every chance that some of Britain's E.F.T.A. partners will join at the same time and that the interests of the Commonwealth can be safeguarded. The implications of political union with Europe, which could involve a loss of sovereignty, are rather more difficult for some to accept. The climate for entry is now extremely favourable, so the country will soon have to make a choice, after the terms of Britain's entry have been negotiated. It will be a choice that will greatly affect the nature of British trade in the future.

Changes in British Shipping

There are visible signs that British shipping is preparing to face the challenge of world competition by a radical reorganization. The government is giving the industry every encouragement to improve, so that British ships will be as advanced in design as possible. Help has been in the form of investment grants,

63 The Tilbury docks are the part of the London docks nearest the sea. In the foreground is the Grain Terminal; the dock behind it is a new extension. Three container bases can be seen. Nearest to the Terminal is the multi-user berth for shipping lines that do not require their own terminal; to the right is the berth used for trade with Australia and on the opposite side is the United States Line berth. The three sheds on the other end of the dock will handle packaged timber and other forest products in unit loads from Sweden and Canada. One of these berths is already in operation.

cheap credit, which was primarily designed to help the shipyards, but also helped the shipowners, and free depreciation, which means that the government makes tax allowances to help with the eventual replacement of the ship once its useful life is finished. The result of this help to invest in new ships is that the average age of British ships is now only six years and they are now newer than most of the world's fleet.

The possession of a modern fleet is important, now that there is a changeover from the conventional cargo liners and tramp steamers to the new bulk carriers and container ships. America was the first to introduce container ships, but although British shipowners were rather suspicious at first, they formed themselves into units to exploit the container earlier than their European rivals. One group of big shipping companies formed Overseas Containers Limited (O.C.L.) in 1965 and another group formed Associated Container Transportation in 1966. These were ready to start operations in 1969, but the opening of their service was stopped by the dockers' unions, which are using the high wages that they can hope to earn at the container bases as a method of raising wages for dockers working on the conventional quays as well.

The result was that the Tilbury terminal, which was the chosen base for Britain's first major container service to Australia, failed to open until 1970. Containers destined for Australia were moved to European ports, and Antwerp was chosen as the terminal, while Tilbury remained shut. This new direction of container traffic brought new life to the eastern ports of England, such as Felixstowe and Harwich, through which containers are fed to the continent. Not all container terminals were closed in this way, but the lesson of Tilbury is that the unions will accept only reluctantly a system of handling, which threatens to cut down the number of jobs in the docks. The container revolution cannot, therefore, be introduced as swiftly and efficiently as the shipowners would like, but it will obviously be the main method of handling goods in the future.

The change in the nature of cargo handling will mean a large reduction in the number of ships needed to service a particular route. It has been estimated that the nine container ships coming into use on the Australia route will replace 50 or 60 conventional ships. The reduction is made possible by the greater speed of the new ships, by the time saved in port and by the ending of the system by which cargo liners called at a number of ports to off-load part of its cargo. This does mean that fewer seamen will be needed in future, but as there is already a shortage and more than 30 per cent of British fleet is manned by Asians, there is little danger of unemployment for for British seamen.

A similar change is apparent on the bulk-shipping side. Large bulk carriers need guaranteed large cargoes if they are to be used efficiently. There was a tendency in the 1960s for British owners to persist with small tramps because they were used to operating from relatively shallow draught British ports and had long-term contracts to rely on. A new approach to bulk shipping has been adopted by the establishment of Seabridge Shipping in 1965. It is really a marketing

64 This is the United States Line's berth at Tilbury. The containers can be seen clearly on the deck of the ship. They are loaded by the huge travelling gantry that moves along the quay on its rails. The special vehicles in the foreground are used to carry the containers to the gantry and are called straddle carriers.

organisation for a number of shipping companies and acts as a centre to which any industrialist, who needs large supplies of ore or fertiliser to be transported by sea, can go. Seabridge can then offer its members large long-term contracts, which will make the use of big bulk carriers worthwhile.

There has, therefore, been a distinct move towards new specialist services in shipping, which will enable large ships to be used efficiently. It puts British shipping a jump ahead of its biggest competitors in Norway, Greece and Liberia, where the fleets are still owned by single men or families. British shipping needs to maintain its competitiveness in this way if Britain is to retain her eminence in world trade.

In the 15th century, Venice led the world, in the 16th century, Portugal, in the 17th century, Holland, but since the 18th century the leader in shipping has been Great Britain. Her superiority was based first on the carriage of bulk products such as timber and coal, and then on her need to maintain worldwide trade as an imperial power. Both the reasons for her superiority have now disappeared. Coal is no longer the major source of power, and the Empire has gradually been given independence. There remains, however, a tradition of seamanship and of trading expertise which has enabled Britain to maintain her superiority, but it would be unrealistic to presume that this lead will persist into the 21st century. Already Japan has a slightly bigger mercantile marine than Britain, and the next century may be hers.

BOOK LIST

The following books are recommended for further reading:

Trading and Travelling, E. H. Dance (Longmans)
Story of Ships, S. E. Ellacott (Methuen)
A Picture Story of Ships, C. Hamilton Ellis (Vista Books)
All About Ships and Shipping, Edwin Harnack (Faber & Faber)
Travel by Sea, R. J. Hoare (Black)
Ships, R. Hope (Batsford)
Transport by Sea, T. Insull (Murray)
Ships, J. S. Murphy (O.U.P.)
Ships and Shipping, J. Penry-Jones (Burke)
The Sailing Ship, R. C. Anderson (Harrap)
Discovering Sailing Ships, C. R. France (U.L.P.)
Sailing Ships, G. S. Laird Clowes (H.M.S.O.)
Merchant Steamers and Motor Ships, H. P. Spratt (H.M.S.O.)
Outline History of Transatlantic Steam Navigation, H. P. Spratt (H.M.S.O.)
British Fishing Boats and Coastal Craft, E. W. White (H.M.S.O.)
Navigation, H. Brinton and P. Moore (Methuen)
Docks and Harbours, Rolt Hammond (Muller)
Docks and Harbours, J. Stewart Murphy (O.U.P.)
Notes on the Port of London (Port of London Authority)
Ships and Cargoes (Port of London Authority)

Index

The numerals in **bold type** refer to the page-numbers of the illustrations.

93